he Opening

nbrier

THE GREENBRIER AND COTTAGES
WHITE SULPHUR SPRINGS

DINNER

Fresh Lobster Supreme 1 25
euvres, Parisienne 1 00   Supreme of Fruit 75   Grapefruit Marashino 50
ons 30   Celery 30   Ripe Olives 40   Olives 30   Smoked Sardines 50
Tin 1 25   Herring or Mackerel in Wine 75   Major Gray Chutney 25
Clam Juice 40   Celery Juice 40   Tomato Juice 40   Sauerkra
e Cod Oysters 50   Bluepoint Oysters 45   Cherry Stone C
Neck Clams 40   Cocktail 10

SOUPS
Oxtail Soup, Printaniere 40   Consomme au
routons 40   Chicken Broth with Rice 40   Clam Br

FISH
ng Dish, Newburg 2 50   Filet of Sole a la
ountain Brook Trout Saute, Meuniere and Potatoes Noise
hesapeake Bay Shad Roe or Shad and Roe with Baco
Creme au Gratin 1 40   Grilled Striped Bass, Sa

ENTREES
ashed Sweet Potatoes 1 25   Sw
ardinal 2 00   Baby Lamb Steak a
d Breast of Chicken with Virginia Ham and   Guinea
quab with Spinach 2 10   Fresh
of New Peas 1 75

ROASTS and BRO
Turkey, Cranberry S   1 75
00   Lamb C

Thanksgiving

The President of The United States

IN HONOR OF

The President of Mexico

AND

The Prime Minister of Canada

The Greenbrier
WHITE SULPHUR SPRINGS

YOU ARE CORDIALLY INVITED
TO COME TO THE ANNUAL
CHILDREN'S PARTY
TUESDAY, AUGUST 25th AT 33
ON THE OLD W
R.S.V.P.

The CS

Crayfish
Ground Mustar
Chardonnay, Greenbrier Vineyard
a Steve Girard Selection, N

Petit Filet Mi
and Smoked Partridge
Sauce Caberne
Michigan White and Green Aspar
Cabernet Sauvignon
Dauphine Pot

The Greenbrier Cookbook

Favorite Recipes From America's Resort

The Greenbrier Cookbook

Favorite Recipes
From America's Resort

Edited by Martha Holmberg
Photography by Ellen Silverman
and Jack Mellott

The Greenbrier
White Sulphur Springs, West Virginia

Published by The Greenbrier

Copyright © 1992 by The Greenbrier

All rights reserved. This book, or any portions thereof, may not be
reproduced without written permission of The Greenbrier.

Edited by Martha Holmberg

Historical text by Robert S. Conte

Design by Rodney Dempsey, Progress Printing

Photography by Ellen Silverman and Jack Mellott

Printed in the United States

Library of Congress Catalog Card Number 92-90305

ISBN 0-9633612-0-1

The Greenbrier
White Sulphur Springs, West Virginia
(304) 536-1110

Table of Contents

A Note From The Editor

In selecting and writing the recipes for this book, our goal was to offer the reader a true taste of The Greenbrier. To this end, we chose a variety of recipes, including "old favorites" that guests have enjoyed consistently throughout the years as well as new dishes that reflect the contemporary nature of our cuisine.

Another aspect of sharing the real Greenbrier cuisine with the reader involved translating the recipes and techniques that are performed by a large team of highly skilled chefs in a vast professional kitchen into recipes that can be efficiently executed by the willing amateur at home. This included scaling down quantities, as well as modifying certain ingredients and techniques to suit the space, time and "staffing" constraints of the non-professional cook. The resulting recipes will produce dishes true to the style and spirit of Greenbrier cuisine—delicious reminders of enjoyable past visits or perhaps temptations to return!

The recipes are written in a style that presents much of the preliminary work as part of the ingredient list, for example cutting vegetables, chopping herbs or softening butter. This makes the recipe text more streamlined, but it also is meant to encourage the cook to work in an orderly fashion in which the preparatory work (the professional term is *mise en place*—literally "put in place") is completed before the actual cooking and assembling of the recipe begins. By having all the ingredients cleaned, peeled, cut and measured, the cook can devote the proper attention to the more challenging and time-sensitive steps in the recipe without risk of confusion or error.

At the back of the book is a Glossary of Basic Recipes, Techniques and Terms. This section will be very helpful in explaining elements in the recipes that may not be familiar. It also will give a useful review of terms that may be very familiar, but nonetheless have specific meanings that are critical to the success of a recipe. Each glossary term is printed in ***bold italic*** the first time it appears in the ingredient list or method of a recipe.

Dedication

Throughout the production of this book, many Greenbrier employees were called upon in various ways, and each one responded with enthusiasm, energy and cooperation. Because of the extraordinary efforts of so many, *The Greenbrier Cookbook* cannot be seen as the product of any individual, but rather it is a collective work enriched by the contributions and talents of the entire Greenbrier staff. It is to them this book is dedicated.

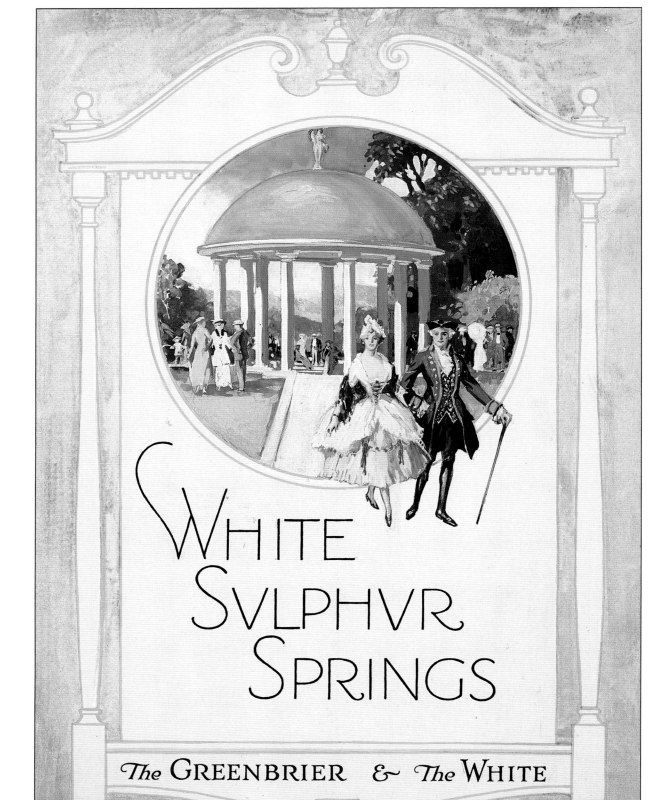

WHITE SVLPHVR SPRINGS

The GREENBRIER & The WHITE

The History of
Dining and Entertaining at

The *Greenbrier*

Over a two-century evolution from rustic log cabins to a grand and gracious resort, The Greenbrier has meant many things to many people. Surely high on the list of anyone's memories would be the experience of fine dining and regal entertaining so characteristic of the place. Today's excellence is the culmination of over two hundred years of proud culinary tradition; the following pages tell the story of that unique heritage.

One of the pivotal events in the history of The Greenbrier took place, appropriately enough, at a dinner party. The dinner, in 1908, was part of a delicately conducted wooing process whereby a small number of prominent West Virginians enticed the man who controlled the Chesapeake and Ohio Railway to add the resort to his portfolio of properties. Among the plotters who engineered the dinner was William Alexander MacCorkle, a former governor of West Virginia.

The target of this maneuvering was Edwin Hawley, who had established a reputation as a no-nonsense businessman—not the kind of man who was interested in rescuing any place more famous for its history than its profitability. Because the resort had been struggling to make even a modest profit for years at that point, it was clear Hawley would require careful handling if MacCorkle and his friends were to succeed.

On that fateful summer evening, MacCorkle escorted Hawley into a private dining room of the Old White—the hotel that stood at White Sulphur Springs before The Greenbrier—and introduced him to the other guests: "We invited many of the beautiful women of the South, and all the stately old men with their courtly air and their beneficent ways," MacCorkle wrote of the event. His idea was to imbue Hawley with a sense of the resort's distinguished heritage and its meaning for generations of Southerners. Thus the conspirators presented what MacCorkle called a "splendid Southern dinner," which he described in loving detail in his memoirs:

> *A mint julep was served in long glasses with the mint eight inches high — a mint julep, as you tasted it, that reminded you of the nectar of Hymettus. A dainty dish of terrapin just from the Chesapeake Bay, prepared with a dash of old Sherry, served along with Madeira sixty years in the wood — verily the sipping of ambrosia. Then came the piece de resistance — a half of canvas-back duck for each plate, cut by a cleaver directly in two, and served with heaping plates of hot Virginia corn dodgers and vegetables fresh from the Company's gardens, while the whole was crowned with golden Champagne.*

The dinner was an inspiration. MacCorkle seized the moment with a toast that celebrated the resort's rich history and then got to the point: "There is one among us who is moved with the sweetness and beauty and the romance of the old place," MacCorkle declared, "and he proposes to touch with his golden wand the Old White, and to bring back its wonderful life." All of the guests rose to their feet and turned to Hawley with glasses raised.

When Hawley acknowledged the salutation, MacCorkle detected the gleam of a tear and knew his strategy had succeeded.

The next morning, Hawley matter-of-factly commented to MacCorkle, "I believe that I will buy this place and turn it over to the Chesapeake and Ohio and rebuild it." And that is just what happened. Within a few years of Hawley's decision, the resort underwent a renaissance: a European-style Bath House featuring a grand indoor swimming pool was complete by 1912; an eighteen-hole golf course and a fine new hotel, The Greenbrier, were open to the fashionable public in 1913.

The stylish scene on The Greenbrier's lawn at afternoon tea is the subject of this 1914 brochure cover artwork.

*T*he resort that MacCorkle's party for Edwin Hawley rescued had been fashionable and famous for well over a century by the time of that dinner. Indeed, 100 years earlier, in 1808, the first permanent building at the resort was completed. Not surprisingly, it was a dining room. That dining room—which stood just about where the croquet lawn is located today—was built to serve travelers along the rough road that traversed the Allegheny Mountains, but more importantly, it served people coming to partake of the sulphur water to restore their health.

The beginning of The Greenbrier's history is traditionally dated by the first recorded use of the White Sulphur Spring in 1778. However, for the next 30 years, accommodations essentially consisted of a few log cabins. People came to "take the waters" to relieve the symptoms of rheumatism, although even as early as 1790 one visitor recalled adding to his saddlebags "a bottle or two of prime French brandy and a pack of cards." Once the primitive road passing by the front of the resort was improved to bear stagecoach traffic, people flocked to White Sulphur Springs, or at least they came in larger numbers than before. By the 1830s crowds of more than 500 were reported.

Although a new dining room was built that accommodated 500, meals in these early days appear to have verged on pandemonium. The most colorful account of meal time at White Sulphur Springs was written by John H.B. Latrobe of Baltimore during his 1832 visit. A clanging bell drew patrons to the dining room, he wrote, and then "every man, woman and child rushes to the seats assigned to them—and in an instant, the viands are snatched, and in another instant, almost, consumed." One particular scene seemed to startle Latrobe: "The day after I arrived, two

The dining room at White Sulphur Springs in 1832, from a painting by John H. B. Latrobe.

waiters quarreled about an apple pie—one floored the other, and neither got the pie, which was also floored in the scuffle."

The problem of service at the table was compounded by a situation that all White Sulphur Springs visitors experienced. Those guests who did not bring servants to act as waiters were forced to rely on what was often called bribery, although other phrases were invented, such as "applying the oil of palms," or "using the soft impeachment of ready change." Again, it was John H. B. Latrobe who said it best: "Bribe high and you live high. Avoid bribery and you starve."

While most of the foodstuffs were bought from outside sources, the resort did possess one great advantage in feeding its guests, namely its location in a region of productive agricultural lands. From the earliest days of settlement, the farms of Greenbrier and Monroe counties produced a bounty of cattle, sheep and hogs. For generations, The Greenbrier has selected the finest beef and lamb as well as chickens, turkeys, maple sugar, and other foods, from the plentiful supply in the area.

Vegetables served to visitors were grown on the property. A grist mill stood on Howard's Creek, a few hundred yards east of today's Golf Clubhouse, where wheat and corn were ground. In the 1840s, the owners purchased 5,000 acres

The Springhouse was always a social center, as well as the source of health-giving mineral water.

including today's golf courses; for over 70 years, however, those wide pastures were used to grow food. For example, most of the Old White Course was grazing land for sheep and cattle, the remaining acreage was in corn and vegetables. Tucked away in a grove of trees near today's sixteenth hole was the slaughter house.

For a century, the ritual of going to drink one's sulphur water at the Springhouse was an integral part of the dining habits of White Sulphur Springs. Before each meal, everyone was expected to gather under the dome and drink three

Today's symbol of The Greenbrier, the Springhouse has graced the center of the grounds since the early 1830s.

glasses of water. People began to congregate about an hour before each meal (the largest quantity of water was consumed before breakfast), and they then wandered up the hill to the dining room, where musicians performed on the veranda until meal service began. These rituals were followed by everyone, even the President of the United States. One journalist noted in 1838: "The President {Martin Van Buren} rides on horseback before breakfast, walks to the springs, eats at the public table with the rest of us, and really begins to be looked upon by the company as a mere man."

Martin Van Buren, one of the 23 presidents who have stayed at The Greenbrier, joined in the social activities much like any other guest during his lengthy visit in 1838.

Though the atmosphere in a professional kitchen today is more relaxed than a century ago, traditional hierarchy and discipline remain the rule. Here, the hectic pace abates long enough for staff to share a meal at the communal chefs' table.

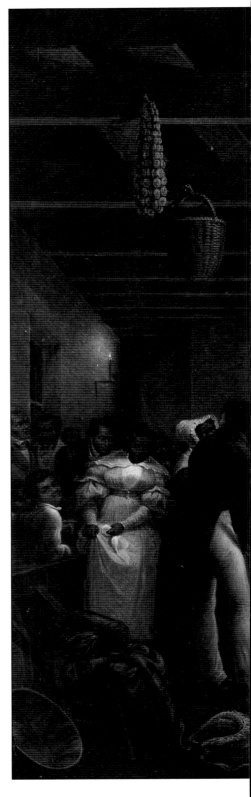

Few descriptions of the kitchen in the nineteenth century survive, but in one, the *chef de cuisine* was by far the most impressive part of the operation: "He seems to have a high sense of his personal and official dignity...all stood aside respectfully to allow free passage to one who, in his sphere, held the place of an emperor."

The writer toured the kitchen on a July morning in 1856 when the chef "had set a-going seventeen simultaneous pans with the fate of seventeen separate breakfasts. Calmly he walked before a roaring furnace that emulated the blast of a foundry...some of the pans were simmering tenderly; some frizzled in a louder key; some rumbled under covers; some, lidless, bubbled full in view. Each had its peculiar crisis and doubtful turning point, yet all these complicated issues his clear mind kept apart." The chef managed his staff with as much skill as he managed the 17 breakfast pans. "Dignified and thoughtful," the writer continued, "he is the very one to legislate with subordinates and overawe waiters. Nobody can brow-beat him, irritate his nerves, or exhaust his patience."

The oldest depiction of dancing at the resort is this painting by Christian Mayr entitled "Kitchen Ball at White Sulphur Springs" from 1838. These are the servants—presumably slaves—holding a festive ball after a long day's labor.

The vast dining room of the Old White Hotel. Over 300 feet long, seating 1,200 guests, this was the largest dining room in the United States in the mid-19th century.

A new and quite large hotel was erected in 1858, and with it began a new era in the resort's history because the first floor of that three-story hotel contained a spacious—indeed gigantic—dining room. The owners proudly trumpeted the fact that, with a capacity of 1,200 people, this was the largest dining room in the United States. It was over 300 feet long, filled with dozens of round tables, each seating at least eight persons. Here was dining on a grand scale!

For the next 64 years, this hotel—which was affectionately called "The White", and in its latter years "The Old White"—was the teeming center of dining and entertaining at White Sulphur Springs. Three times a day the company from the hotel and cottages took their assigned seats in the vast dining room. A hotel and dining room on this scale were necessary because the annual summertime crowd was due to increase with the arrival of a powerful new force in American life — the railroad. The Civil War delayed completion of the railroad until 1869, but once the resort reopened (after use by both sides during the war), the railroad breathed new life into what was already an historic American place.

The railroad also connected the resort to sources of food that had been out of reach during the earlier stagecoach days. The mountain resort became linked to the seaboard, and therefore to imported items. In the past, fruits had been a luxury, and fish were fresh-water only; but by the 1870s, recent rarities such as oranges, lemons, pineapples and bananas were available. The railroad that served White

After the Civil War, the resort's letterhead highlighted its location on the main line of the Chesapeake and Ohio Railroad.

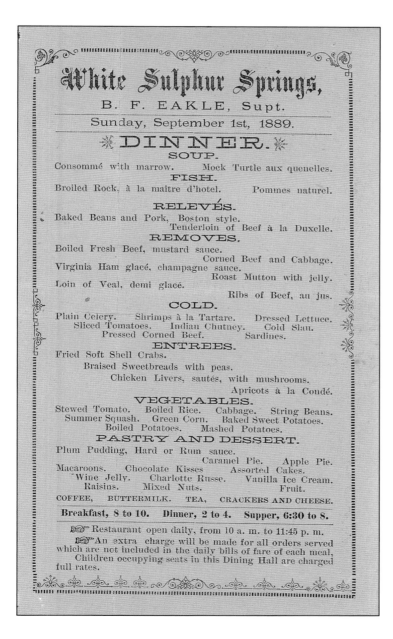

A typical dinner menu in the 1880s. Note that this meal was served from 2:00 to 4:00 p.m.

The entire staff of the Old White's dining room gathered on the hotel's front steps about 1890.

Postcards, like this one showing an afternoon lawn party in 1891, were attached to each day's menu for diners to tear off and use as souvenirs.

Sulphur Springs—the Chesapeake and Ohio—brought to the resort the legendary bounty of the Chesapeake Bay region. Grain from the western states and tea from overseas were supplied by rail. Beef transported by railroad tasted better, it was said, because it was less "travel-weary". Items such as Indian chutney, lobster, soft-shell crab, salmon, sea turtle, clams, apricots, blueberries, strawberries and shrimp began to supplement traditional items on the resort's menus.

Dinner was by far the largest meal of the day, and it was served between two and four in the afternoon. It followed the busiest time of the day, the late morning and early afternoon, when activities bustled out on the great lawn where croquet and lawn tennis tournaments were held. Three days a week guests danced around a Victorian bandstand at high noon, and on the other days joined in cham-

The Springhouse as it looked about 1910.

pagne and fruit parties under the branches of huge white oak trees.

From all reports, the service at meals had changed since the rough and tumble beginnings in the original dining room. A correspondent for a Charleston, South Carolina newspaper commented that "the White Sulphur is probably the only fashionable resort where life does not materially depend for its support on the bribes given to the waiters." Surely matters had improved dramatically over the years.

If the mid-day meal was the grand dining experience, the evening meal, interchangeably referred to as either "supper" or "tea," was more sedate and

The main entrance of The Greenbrier Hotel shortly after it opened in September of 1913.

functioned as the prelude to dancing in the ballroom. Indeed, evening tea—which featured hot breads, fruits, cakes, perhaps eggs and some cold meats—was the staging area for the nightly display of costumes.

Though the merry seasons continued into the early years of the twentieth century, financial problems at the resort seemed to preordain a bleak future. At least that was how it appeared until William MacCorkle and friends came up with the idea of the Chesapeake and Ohio Railway's buy-out and sold Edwin Hawley on the proposal at the famous dinner of 1908.

Within a few years of the railroad's purchase, over $2 million had been invested at White Sulphur Springs to create a year-round, world-class resort. Most of that money went into building The Greenbrier Hotel, which opened in the fall of 1913. To celebrate the hotel's opening, the president of the C&O hosted a dinner for 100 members of the press in the new dining room, which was laden with thousands of roses for the occasion. *The New York Times* described it as "a delightful dinner elegantly served, beyond which nothing could be desired."

Virtually unrecognizable today, this is what the main dining room looked like from 1913 to 1930.

*T*n the years before World War II, a German chef, Ernest Schleussener, reigned in the kitchen, and the majority of his staff was European. This was also true in the dining room, where most of the waiters and captains were from Germany, Austria and Switzerland. Frequently, these personnel worked at The Greenbrier on a seasonal basis and spent the remainder of the year rotating among other resorts and urban hotels up and down the Eastern seaboard.

Three chefs stepped outside for this photograph in 1914.

The Bath Department reflected a European influence, too, offering "A European Cure in America." Treatments in the new facilities were modeled on those developed at the famous and ancient spas of Europe, and included an emphasis on cuisine. Dr. George Kahlo (the physician in charge of the Bath Department) wrote, "One of the most important features of the 'Cure' is the regulation of the diet." Therefore a special diet kitchen was created, "from which may be obtained," he explained with an unfortunate choice of words, "a great variety of foods suitable to almost every disease." This attention to diet led to separate menus, as noted in a spa brochure: "In addition to the regular menu, which is prepared to meet the desires of cosmopolitan visitors of luxurious habits, there is a special diet menu. Table d'hôte luncheons and dinners are served from both."

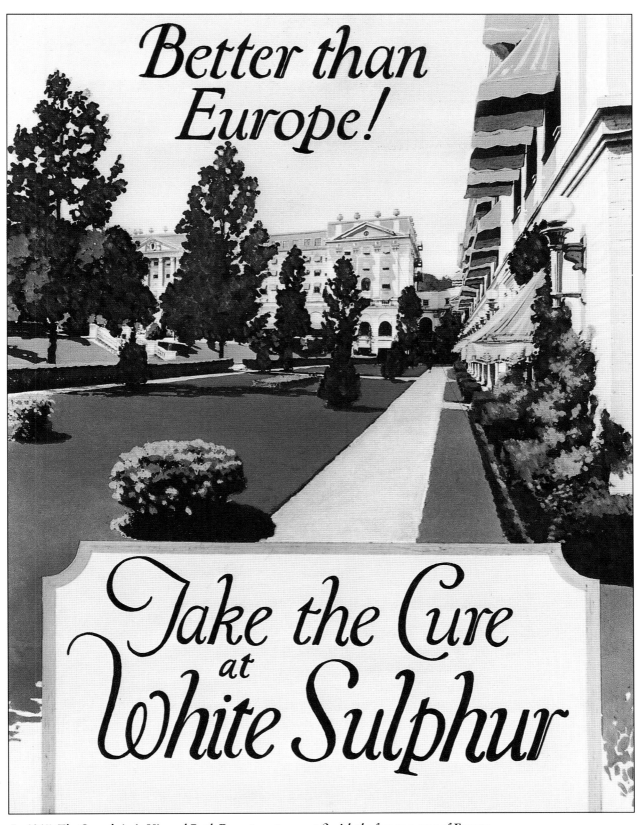

In 1915, The Greenbrier's Mineral Bath Department competed with the famous spas of Europe.

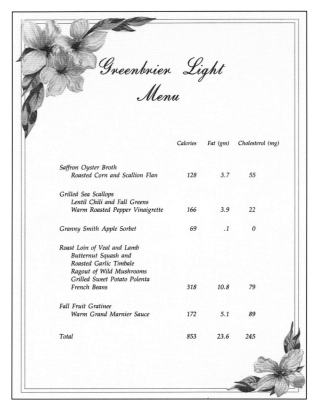

Greenbrier Light Menu

	Calories	Fat (gm)	Cholesterol (mg)
Saffron Oyster Broth			
Roasted Corn and Scallion Flan	128	3.7	55
Grilled Sea Scallops			
Lentil Chili and Fall Greens			
Warm Roasted Pepper Vinaigrette	166	3.9	22
Granny Smith Apple Sorbet	69	.1	0
Roast Loin of Veal and Lamb			
Butternut Squash and			
Roasted Garlic Timbale			
Ragout of Wild Mushrooms			
Grilled Sweet Potato Polenta			
French Beans	318	10.8	79
Fall Fruit Gratinee			
Warm Grand Marnier Sauce	172	5.1	89
Total	853	23.6	245

Today's health-conscious guest can select meals from Spa and Greenbrier Light menus.

This interest in healthy eating, which might be assumed to be a modern preoccupation, extended beyond the scope of the spa and into the general body of resort guests. The writer Harrison Rhodes wrote in 1915, "Luxury and pleasure are, of course, never out of fashion; what is to be noted is the present tremendous vogue of health." He was unsure how to explain this phenomenon—"It may be because all gowns are so unreticent nowadays," he speculated—but The Greenbrier fit a pattern he saw across the country while writing *In Vacation America*. "Red meat and rich sauces, champagne and burgundy are gradually disappearing from the highest and gayest tables," he noted. "There are fashionable seasons of the year when nobody who is anybody eats more than a slice of the breast of chicken and fresh green peas, or drinks more than a cool cup of water from the spring."

A desire for healthful living motivated just about everyone out to the new golf and tennis facilities, which were extremely popular in the trendy spring and autumn seasons. Tennis courts were in play near the new golf clubhouse, and in 1913 The Greenbrier could boast both an entertaining nine-hole golf course and a nationally recognized eighteen-hole course. The clubhouse itself, cheerfully called The Casino, became a stylish luncheon spot and one more scene for afternoon tea. These afternoon tea gatherings, which featured lively dancing, were often farewell parties for guests departing to New York to sail for Europe.

Another busy dining and entertaining spot was Kate's Mountain Lodge. The original lodge (which opened in 1918 and was replaced in 1957) was a rustic log building where lunch was served daily on a veranda

A 1914 Town and Country *magazine feature story about fashionable ladies' wear on The Greenbrier's golf links included this charming photograph.*

Kates Mountain Club   White Sulphur Springs, W. Va.

The original Kate's Mountain Lodge was built in 1918 and torn down in 1957.

with a spectacular view of the Allegheny Mountains in every direction. In the evenings, the lodge was a favorite location for private parties and dinners, and in keeping with its unpretentious setting, meals at Kate's Mountain were fairly straightforward. A typical menu began with Creole Soup, and then offered Southern Fried Chicken with yams, spoon corn bread, string bean salad and cheese.

Although Kate's Mountain was a country lodge, it was the scene of formal dinners and masquerade parties, and it was the place to stop for lunch while on day-long horseback rides over some of The Greenbrier's two hundred miles of

Scenic Allegheny Mountain vistas frame the outdoor entertaining areas at today's Kate's Mountain Lodge.

Despite the rustic interior, meals at Kate's Mountain Lodge in the 1920s were served on fine china.

trails. Hunting parties left the lodge for all-night chases which culminated at dawn with roasted raccoon ("considered a delicacy," one writer reported). Every Sunday a buffet was featured in the evening, then guests rode down the mountain to an orchestra concert in the hotel's main lobby.

In the twenties, The Greenbrier was definitely the resort of choice for the people newspaper columnists described as "prominent smart-setters." Society scribe Cholly Knickerbocker declared, "The Easter parade down Fifth Avenue has been undercut by golf and the motor car as society people head south to White Sulphur Springs." These fashionable crowds filled the hotel and cottages to capacity not only at Easter, but over other holidays as well, and during the annual horse show in August. The Old White Hotel was reluctantly torn down in 1922, and several years later The Greenbrier Hotel expanded dramatically to accommodate its ever-increasing clientele. By the spring of 1931, when work was complete, the hotel's capacity was nearly doubled with the additions of the North Wing and the Virginia Wing.

This virtual rebuilding of the hotel created today's Main Dining Room by extending the building to the south. Though the decorating scheme in the dining room has changed over the years, the basic size and structure has not. Ever since, one of the fundamental delights of life at The Greenbrier has been striding to one's table under high ceilings, past rows of columns, and flanked on either side by tremendous Georgian windows. In one section, the chandeliers glowing down upon

The main dining room of The Greenbrier, in 1934 at left and in 1992 at right.

the diners have graced the room since 1931. Another facet of this expansion was enlarging the dining area in the Golf Clubhouse so that "al fresco" dining on the porch featured a panoramic view of the golf courses, while on the other side, lunch on what was called the Terrace spread between the clubhouse and the tennis courts.

The Greenbrier was able to maintain its standards of refinement and hospitality even through the Great Depression. Throughout the 1930s, music festivals, golf and tennis tournaments and special holiday productions were held, but the biggest event each year was Robert E. Lee Week. Here was the grandest historical

The porch of the Golf Clubhouse has been a popular luncheon spot since the building opened in 1915. This photograph was taken about 1933.

pagentry ever staged at The Greenbrier. To honor General Lee's visits to White Sulphur Springs after the Civil War, the last week in August was filled with dancing, trips to historic sites, morning lawn parties and numerous classic Southern meals.

Also during the 1930s, meetings of business and professional groups became a larger part of the annual guest count at The Greenbrier, as they did throughout the hotel industry. During those years, The Greenbrier evolved into an exclusive gathering place for the leaders of the steel, railroad, automobile, banking, utilities, insurance, finance and coal industries. For the world of dining and entertaining, this meant more private dinners and banquets, some of which were held in the Main Dining Room and others in a combination auditorium/dining room known as Governors' Hall (which was later transformed into the Crystal Dining Room).

Everyone was in full costume for The Old White Fancy Dress Ball in 1935, an annual event from 1932 to 1941.

Chesapeake and Ohio Railway President Walter Tuohy hosted this Christmas party in the Crystal Room in 1962.

When The Greenbrier was converted into an Army hospital during World War II, the main dining room became a particularly elegant mess hall.

The social whirl at The Greenbrier came to a sudden halt with the declaration of war following the attack on Pearl Harbor in December, 1941. For the duration of World War II, The Greenbrier was in government service, first leased by the U.S. State Department as a temporary home for foreign diplomats and then purchased by the U.S. Army and converted into a 2,000-bed hospital.

From December 1941 to July 1942, The Greenbrier was closed to the public, and instead housed hundreds of German, Japanese and Italian diplomats, along with their spouses and children. During that time, all the members of these various groups were treated as regular Greenbrier guests: staff size, meals and service remained the same. This continued until negotiations were completed to exchange these foreign diplomats for American diplomats interned overseas.

The Army renamed The Greenbrier to honor one of its own, Dr. Bailey K. Ashford. This pamphlet explained the facilities to each soldier admitted to the hospital.

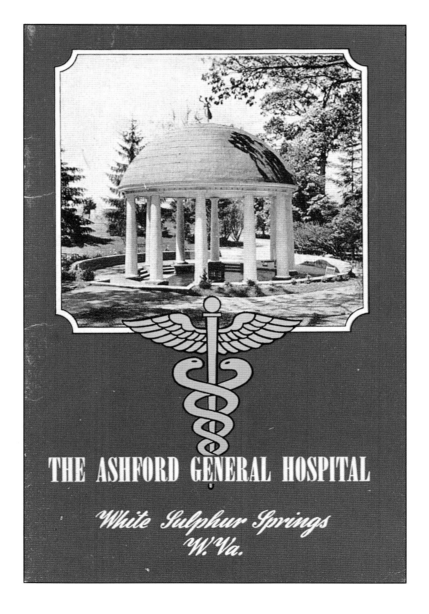

THE ASHFORD GENERAL HOSPITAL

White Sulphur Springs W. Va.

Because of the large number of Europeans on The Greenbrier's kitchen and dining room staff, employees were closely checked by the FBI during this period. Although it is doubtful that FBI agents actually donned waiter's uniforms and listened in on dinner conversations among the diplomats, members of the hotel staff were discreetly questioned for any information they may have acquired through contact with the diplomatic party.

Before the last diplomat left, the U.S. Army began proceedings to take over the entire resort for use as a surgical center and base hospital. In the four years when The Greenbrier was Ashford General Hospital (from 1942 to 1946), 25,000 soldiers were admitted and treated. The hotel became the hospital: guest rooms were converted into wards and the Main Dining Room was the Mess Hall. The private dining rooms (now called the Washington and Lee Rooms) were filled with temporary bookshelves bearing the hospital's medical library. Kate's Mountain Lodge functioned as an NCO Club, and officers used the Golf Clubhouse as a Lounge.

All the resort's facilities were used by the recuperating soldiers—golf, tennis, indoor swimming pool, hiking trails, mineral baths, etc. To assist in the operation of a hospital on this scale, many former employees of The Greenbrier became part of the civilian service personnel. This was especially true in the Mess Kitchen, where these civilians were supplemented by German prisoners of war. Here is one of those incongruities brought about by wartime: in the kitchens of Ashford General Hospital were hardened veterans of Field Marshall Rommel's elite North Africa Corps helping prepare meals for wounded American servicemen. Incidentally, The Greenbrier's head chef was not hired by the Army. Apparently, it was clear after a brief interview that he was not going to be able to make the transition from Greenbrier cuisine to military cuisine.

After the war, the Chesapeake and Ohio Railway bought back The Greenbrier and embarked upon a total redecoration of the hotel and property under the leadership of a legendary interior decorator, Dorothy Draper. Much of her work, which began in late 1946, is still evident at The Greenbrier today. For example, most of the china used in the dining rooms bears a Dorothy Draper design, the portraits of eighteenth and nineteenth century American dignitaries in the Main Dining Room were selected by Dorothy Draper and the chandelier that crowns the red and pink Cameo Ballroom is a Dorothy Draper custom creation. Her brilliant colors brought new life to The Greenbrier's interior spaces, setting the scene for thousands of dinners, parties and receptions ever since.

A 1948 advertisement in **The New Yorker** *magazine.*

press people, also carefully selected. Everyone who was anyone was at The Greenbrier that third week in April — representatives of old-line Southern society, stars from Hollywood, a smattering of royalty, a half-dozen members of the Kennedy clan, Grace Kelly's parents from Philadelphia, and (to quote one clever society watcher) "the Palm Beach, Newport, and Tuxedo crowd in a state of deep tan."

Called "the greatest gathering of society ever held in this country" by the *New York Herald Tribune*, it was the kind of

Dorothy Draper completed her top-to-bottom redecoration in April of 1948 just in time for the most famous event in the resort's long history, a lavish party celebrating the reopening of The Greenbrier, hosted by Robert R. Young, Chairman of the C&O Railway. The carefully selected guests had free rein of the property and their every move was covered by a cadre of

Dorothy Draper selected the early nineteenth century American portraits that still hang on the walls of The Greenbrier's main dining room.

Bob Hope presents the Duke and Duchess of Windsor with a bottle of champagne for winning the annual Waltz Contest at the 1953 Spring Festival.

This photograph is from Life magazine's coverage of "the Big Weekend at White Sulphur" in 1948. The hostess for the party was Mrs. Robert R. Young (with parasol).

party where even veteran socialites and celebrities were startled to hear Bing Crosby croon several tunes accompanied by a band that included the Duke of Windsor on the drums!

The reopening party was such a success that it was repeated each May and was called the Spring Festival. Scheduled the week after the Kentucky Derby, the party at Churchill Downs simply moved down the line of the C & O to The Greenbrier. For a decade, the stars of this event were the Duke and Duchess of Windsor. No one since then has so personified international "High Society" as they did. The former King of England and his American wife, according to one who frequently witnessed their Greenbrier entrances, never failed to electrify the crowd.

Like any Greenbrier party, the Festival included golf tournaments; the host for these outings was the inimitable Sam Snead who was the resort's pro for

Sam Snead wonders if there is any future on the golf course for The Greenbrier's Executive Chef in this 1951 photograph.

decades. Challenging golf in the daytime, followed by fine dining and sophisticated dancing in the evening, these ingredients of the Spring Festival have remained the paradigm for any gathering at The Greenbrier for many years now.

The glittering scene at The Diamond Ball climaxed the famous 1948 party celebrating the reopening of The Greenbrier.

*I*n 1955 Hermann Rusch was selected to fill the position of Executive Food Director at The Greenbrier. His appointment marked a dramatic progression in the culinary evolution of The Greenbrier, which ultimately led to the refined style and world-renowned status of today's cuisine. An important legacy of his years as the Food Director is his innovative administrative decision to create The Greenbrier's famed Culinary Apprenticeship Program. The program was implemented to solve two related staffing problems in The Greenbrier's kitchen. One was high turnover among European chefs, who often came to the resort with only a hazy understanding of American geography—that is, they traveled to White Sulphur Springs assuming it was a few miles down the road from Manhattan. Rusch found that too many chefs established their credentials at The Greenbrier and then moved on. On the other hand, there was no place in the United States where an American could learn classic culinary techniques and cuisine. The Greenbrier's Culinary Apprenticeship Program, which began in 1957, was designed to provide the resort with a highly trained and stable staff and it accomplished that goal quickly.

The Greenbrier's 2-year Culinary Apprenticeship Program culminates in a demanding practical examination. Students receive a "mystery basket" of random ingredients from which they must design and execute a 5-course meal that meets the exacting standards of the panel of judges, headed by program founder Hermann Rusch.

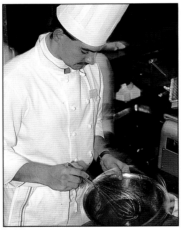

The Culinary Apprenticeship Program continues today. By 1992 more than 200 students had graduated from a course of study that demands a minimum of two years of both classroom work and on-the-job training. Perhaps the best evidence of the program's success is that the person selected to replace Rusch upon his

retirement in 1977, Rodney G. Stoner, is himself a graduate of the program, and currently serves as the hotel's Director of Food and Beverage. Certainly what young culinarians find attractive about the program (hundreds of applications are routinely received for about 10 openings each year) is the tremendous range of experience offered working at The Greenbrier.

While all this attention was paid to back-of-the-house training and organization, a corresponding upgrading of dining facilities continued. The first major banquet room—the Chesapeake Room—opened in 1954. With decor by Dorothy Draper, here was an appropriate setting for the increasing number of large private dinners brought about by the swelling number of conference guests. In the post-war years, group business increased throughout the hotel and resort industry, and The Greenbrier responded by skillfully blending new facilities into the established ambiance of the place. By the early 1970s, the Chesapeake Room was too small to serve the growing business and professional associations (many of which had been meeting for decades at The Greenbrier), and to meet their needs Colonial Hall opened in 1974.

Much of the dining and entertaining that is such an important part of The Greenbrier goes on in smaller, more intimate settings. For that reason, the historic cottages of South Carolina, Tansas and Baltimore Rows were expanded, modernized and enlarged in the 1970s and 1980s. There is no more traditional place to entertain at The Greenbrier than the porch of one of these cottages, where mint julep parties were the fashion long before the Civil War.

Another cottage on the grounds is the one built by Edwin Hawley shortly after he saved The Greenbrier by investing railroad money in the resort. For the last forty years, Hawley Cottage has been the home of three presidents of The Greenbrier, including the current President and Managing Director, Ted J. Kleisner. In June of 1991, a dinner in honor of former British Prime Minister Margaret Thatcher was hosted by Mr. and Mrs. Kleisner in Hawley Cottage.

Clearly the most spectacular renovation occurred in 1989 when the Colonnade cottage was transformed into a three-bedroom, two-parlor Estate

The dining room of the Colonnade estate house is often the venue for formal dinners with up to 24 guests.

House featuring a magnificent dining room. Around a mahogany table are 24 exquisite Prince of Wales style Sheridan chairs, creating one of the most formal dining settings at The Greenbrier. Because Martin Van Buren was a guest in the cottage (the president's son married the daughter of the man who built the Colonnade in 1838), the table is set with china reproduced from the pattern President Van Buren used in the White House.

Many of the Tavern Room's contemporary American specialties are cooked in the rotisserie.

In contrast to these locations for private entertaining, two restaurants created in the 1970s augment service in the Main Dining Room. As part of an expansion of the Old White Club, an entirely new dining area, the Tavern Room, was created. In twenty years this dining room has developed its own distinctive and refined style of sumptuous American dining. Then the Golf Clubhouse was doubled in size, and the porch overlooking the three golf courses—which had been a popular luncheon spot for sixty years at that point—was enclosed, framing a stunning view of the sun setting over the Allegheny Mountains.

In addition to servicing regular dining and banquet operations, there are extraordinary times when the culinary brigade is challenged by the presence of dignitaries or by unique circumstances. Over the years The Greenbrier's staff has not infrequently been asked to prepare meals for presidents, prime ministers and royalty. And though the mix of guests may be international, The Greenbrier prefers to emphasize its historic American roots in these menus. A good example is the sampling of specialties served on the occasion of President Eisenhower's 1956 North American Summit Conference with the president of Mexico, Adolfo Cortines, and the prime minister of Canada, Louis St. Laurent. The president wanted a friendly meeting—he thought of it as inviting neighbors over for dinner. The meals served over a three-day period reflected the best of this country's regional specialties, including Key West green turtle soup, Maine lobster, Philadelphia brie cheese, Kentucky Bibb lettuce, Everglades frog legs, Carolina rice, Maryland crabcakes, brandied Georgia peaches, California pears and Tenderloin of Black Angus Beef.

While enjoying the casual atmosphere of the restaurant at the Golf Clubhouse, diners can survey the activity on the driving range and the resort's 3 golf courses.

President Eisenhower with his guests Adolfo Cortines, the president of Mexico (left), and Louis St. Laurent, the prime minister of Canada, in March, 1956.

Twenty-four karat gold gives the Gold Service base plates a rich burnished glow.

For those who may not be royalty but merely want to dine like royalty, The Greenbrier offers the Gold Service Dinner. This service began in 1956 when the resort purchased special settings of Syracuse China, International Silver and Steuben crystal designed with The Greenbrier logo and trimmed in 24 karat gold. The first Gold Service Dinner was President Eisenhower's State Dinner, which was the culmination of his North American Summit Conference. Today there are some 200 place settings in the kitchen's inventory. At first, these pieces were used quite rarely, mostly at dinners hosted by officials of the C & O Railway.

The Cameo Ballroom was the site of a gala Gold Service Dinner held in December 1991 for the CSX Board of Directors. The ballroom's decor, including the 3,000-piece crystal chandelier, was designed by Dorothy Draper in 1948.

One early Gold Service dinner was a rather unusual event in the political climate of the 1950s, when an American businessman, Cyrus Eaton, hosted the Soviet ambassador to the United States to dinner in the Presidential Suite. In hindsight, Eaton's reasoning for bringing the ambassador to this particular place was quite prophetic: "The Greenbrier makes a favorable impression on Communists," he said, "because it is probably the most capitalistic spot in America."

Special dining arrangements at The Greenbrier are not limited to changes of china and crystal, however. In September 1979, The Greenbrier was the site of the International Ryder Cup Matches and 20,000 golf fans converged on White Sulphur Springs. For a week, the Indoor Tennis Center undertook a new mission as a temporary dining room. On another occasion, a large financial institution rented an entire circus for their entertainment. A tent was erected for the performance, during which dinner for 600 was served. For two evenings, Greenbrier waiters paraded to their tables not under crystal chandeliers but under the canvas big top.

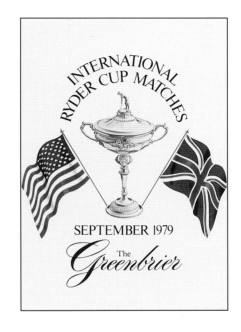

The program from the 1979 Ryder Cup, one of the golf world's premier tournaments since 1927.

The Greenbrier was home to some very unusual guests during the special circus event organized for a conference group.

A table set in the dining room of a 1926 private railroad car—originally named the "St. Nicholas"—now stationed on a siding across from The Greenbrier's main gate.

Hotel and resort industry executives reserve especially elaborate welcomes for those times when they host their peers. When the other winners of the prestigious Mobil Five-Star Award traveled to The Greenbrier in April of 1985 for the awards ceremony, it was not only by train, but in a collection of private railroad cars the likes of which hadn't been seen together for half a century. The specially assembled train carried representatives of the finest hotels, resorts and restaurants in America from Alexandria, Virginia to White Sulphur Springs with champagne flowing and splendid box lunches for all. (Here, however, was an instance when the term "box lunch" was a significant understatement.)

Traveling to The Greenbrier by rail is the historically correct way to reach the resort. For five consecutive years in the 1980s, The Greenbrier was the site of the Democratic Issues Conference, when Democratic members of the House of Representatives, their families, staff, press and sponsors boarded The Congressional Special in Washington's magnificent Union Station for the trip to West Virginia.

A waiter prepares beverages on a vintage luggage cart for a reception to be held outside The Greenbrier train station.

These rail journeys constituted the largest movements of members of Congress in U.S. history. They also meant serving 800 meals (each way) stretched out over 20 Amtrak cars, a task carried out by a crew of experienced Greenbrier room service waiters.

Because of the long-standing relationship between The Greenbrier and the adjacent railroad (the C & O Railway is now part of CSX, a company that operates one of the largest railroads in the United States and is the owner of the resort), it is appropriate that a new dining location opened in 1990 in the 60-year-old train station. Designed for use by small private groups, dinners and receptions are held inside the station—which has been decorated with Greenbrier-related railroad memorabilia—but part of the unique setting is the four historic private railroad cars parked next to the station. These extraordinary cars from the 1920s and 1930s remain in mint condition because they were used as railroad office cars for decades

Dorothy Draper's design legacy continues in Draper's Cafe, opened in 1990.

Specially designed table accessories contribute to the charm of Draper's Cafe. The ceramic watermelon sugar bowls are reproductions of a party favor given to guests at the 1948 reopening party.

after their private ownership. In fact, one of the cars is still used by CSX to entertain clients. This car is often taken to Washington, D.C. where a Greenbrier chef prepares the meal in the car's kitchen and Greenbrier personnel serve in its mahogany-paneled dining room.

Back in White Sulphur Springs, another long-standing relationship was honored when Draper's Cafe opened its doors for the first time in April of 1990. Here is an entirely new restaurant serving breakfast, lunch and afternoon tea, which is available for private evening functions as well. The Cafe is named for Dorothy Draper, and though she died in 1969, her company continues, headed by her successor Carleton Varney. The company she founded still decorates The Greenbrier, and the Cafe is a tribute to her both in its stylish decor (a salute from Carleton Varney to his mentor), and in the items offered on the menu, some of which reflect her personal favorites when she entertained at home.

Over the years, many guests have wanted to take a bit of their Greenbrier culinary experience into their own homes. With this in mind, the first resort cooking school in America was inaugurated at The Greenbrier in 1977. For 15 years, the reputation of this school grew rapidly under the leadership of culinary instructor and author Julie Dannenbaum, and the school became nationally recognized within the culinary industry. Hundreds of professional and non-professional chefs delighted in the school's variety of ideas and techniques. Upon Julie Dannenbaum's retirement, The Greenbrier announced another first— bringing the distinguished Ecole de Cuisine La Varenne of France, directed by Anne Willan, to the resort. 1991 was, to say the least, a terrifically successful debut season for "La Varenne at The Greenbrier". Here was a wise merger of culinary experience: the legendary resources of The Greenbrier's kitchens combined with Anne Willan's 25 years of teaching and writing about food.

Guest chef Jean-Michel Bouvier at La Varenne at The Greenbrier Cooking School shares his secrets of la cuisine francaise.

Julie Dannenbaum

Anne Willan

The story of The Greenbrier is one of evolution and adaptability resulting in a unique personality immediately evident to a guest of the resort. In dining service and entertaining style, The Greenbrier's historical antecedents are very much in evidence: the deep-seated heritage of Southern hospitality, the health-wise ways of European spas and the sporty lifestyle of American country clubs. Mix in a culinary staff versed in the finest gastronomical traditions and hundreds of employees typifying the friendliness and generosity of West Virginia, and you have the ingredients that make The Greenbrier one-of-a-kind.

Hors d'Oeuvres & Appetizers

SUN-DRIED TOMATO AND CHEVRE DIP

This easy recipe makes a splendid dip for crudités or crackers.

¹/₂ cup sun-dried tomatoes

8 ounces cream cheese, softened
at room temperature

8 ounces fresh *chevre* cheese,
softened at room temperature

1 small clove garlic, minced

Salt and freshly ground black
pepper, to taste

1. Soak the tomatoes in very hot water until they are plump and soft, about 20 minutes. (If using tomatoes packed in oil, skip this step.) Drain off excess water or oil and finely chop the tomatoes.

2. Place the cheeses, tomatoes and garlic in a food processor and work until well-blended (alternatively, mix well with a wooden spoon). Season to taste with salt and pepper. Transfer to a small bowl. Serve the dip with fresh vegetables or crackers, or use it as a filling for hollowed-out vegetables such as cherry tomatoes, snow peas and cucumber cups.

Makes 1¹/₂ cups

DRAPER'S CAFE CRABMEAT AND SAGA FRITTERS

Serve these savory fritters straight from the fryer — they are excellent dipped in Spicy Remoulade Sauce (page 88).

1 cup all-purpose flour

6 eggs, separated

1/2 cup milk

8 ounces Saga or other mild blue cheese, rind removed

8 ounces cooked lump crabmeat, picked through to remove any shell

Salt and freshly ground black pepper, to taste

Oil (such as canola, soy or safflower), for deep-frying

1. Put the flour in a medium bowl and make a well in the center. Put the egg yolks and the milk in the well and whisk to combine the wet ingredients thoroughly, using small strokes to draw in very little flour at a time. Bit by bit increase the size of the stroke to blend in more flour without making lumps. When the mixture has formed a smooth batter, crumble in the cheese and the crabmeat, stirring until just combined. Season generously with salt and pepper, to taste. (Remember that the cheese is salty, but the egg whites are bland.)

2. With an electric mixer or by hand with a whisk, whip the egg whites in a large bowl until they form soft peaks. Carefully fold the 2 mixtures together.

3. Heat the oil in a large heavy saucepan or deep-fryer to 375F. (Do not fill the pan more than half-full with oil, as it will foam up when batter is added. Use a thermometer to regulate the temperature.) With a spoon or an ice cream scoop, spoon out 1/8 cup of the fritter batter and drop into the hot oil. Fry until puffed and deep golden brown, about 3 minutes. Drain on paper towels and serve immediately.

Makes about 3 dozen fritters

STEAK TARTARE

A classic canape that's great as a first course, too. Use only top-quality meat and keep the tartare icy-cold until ready to serve.

1/4 cup finely *diced* onion

3 anchovy filets, well-drained and finely chopped

1 egg yolk

1 tablespoon chopped fresh parsley

1 teaspoon ketchup

1 teaspoon salt

1 teaspoon Worcestershire sauce

1 teaspoon well-drained chopped capers

1/2 teaspoon freshly ground black pepper

1/2 teaspoon prepared Dijon mustard

1/4 teaspoon wine vinegar or brandy

Few drops Tabasco sauce

1 pound beef tenderloin or sirloin, trimmed of all fat and gristle and cut into cubes

More chopped parsley

1. Combine the first twelve ingredients in a large bowl and stir well with a fork, mashing the onions, capers and anchovies.

2. Grind the beef in a meat grinder set on coarse. Alternatively, chop the beef in a food processor, using the pulse button to avoid overworking, or chop by hand with a knife. (Whichever method you use, the meat should retain a slightly coarse texture.) Add the chopped meat to the seasonings and blend well with a spoon and fork. Taste and correct the seasoning. Mound the tartare in a small chilled bowl, top with a pinch of chopped parsley and serve with melba toast or buttered rye bread toast. For canapes, shape 2 teaspoons of the tartare into a ball, arrange on crackers or croutons and decorate with chopped parsley.

Serves 8 as a first course or makes about 4 dozen canapes

SMOKED SALMON TARTARE

Everyone loves smoked salmon with aperitifs. This recipe puts a twist on it with some piquant accents.

1 pound skinless smoked salmon, trimmed of any grayish flesh and checked for bones

Juice of 1 lemon, or to taste

2 tablespoons finely *diced* onions

2 tablespoons finely chopped hard-boiled egg white

2 tablespoons chopped fresh parsley

1 tablespoon chopped capers

1 teaspoon extra-virgin olive oil

4 drops Tabasco sauce, or to taste

1. Chop the salmon with a large knife until finely minced. Alternatively, chop in the food processor using the pulse button. (Take care not to overwork; the salmon should retain a slightly coarse texture.)

2. Combine the chopped salmon with the remaining ingredients. Taste and correct seasoning. Serve as a first course with toast points and a lemon wedge, or on crackers or croutons as a canape.

Serves 8 as a first course or makes about 4 dozen canapes

Pictured above: Steak Tartare, Smoked Salmon Tartare, Brandied Chicken Livers

BRANDIED CHICKEN LIVERS

This recipe has been around the hotel for a long time; recently we've given it a new twist by serving it with fresh poached pear. Keeping the chicken livers slightly pink in the center will enhance the sweet flavor of this rich spread.

1/2 cup chopped onion
(1/2 medium onion)

8 tablespoons (1 stick)
unsalted butter

8 ounces chicken livers,
trimmed of any yellow spots,
fat and membrane

2 tablespoons sherry

4 tablespoons brandy

1/2 cup heavy cream

Salt and freshly ground black
pepper, to taste

1. In a medium sauté pan, *sauté* the onions in the butter until soft but not brown, 3-4 minutes. Add the chicken livers and the sherry; season with salt and pepper. Cover and *simmer* over low heat until the livers are pink in the center, 3-4 minutes. Transfer to a bowl and chill the mixture until the butter has solidified, at least 4 hours.

2. Place the cold chicken liver mixture and the brandy in a food processor or blender and blend until very smooth. Pass through a sieve to remove any remaining lumps, if desired. Stir in the cream, then taste and correct seasoning. Chill again until the mixture is firm enough to spread or pipe before serving. Serve with melba toast, rounds of French bread, or pipe it onto half a poached pear to serve as a first course.

Makes about 3 dozen canapes

GRAVLAX

*The Greenbrier gives some Southern zip to this Scandinavian-inspired salmon dish
by adding a shot of bourbon! Partially freezing the finished gravlax will facilitate slicing.*

1 1/2 **pounds salmon filet, skin on,
all bones removed**

1/4 **cup roughly chopped fresh dill**

1/4 **cup roughly chopped
fresh tarragon**

1 **teaspoon rinsed and crushed
green peppercorns**

1/4 **cup kosher salt**

1/2 **cup granulated sugar**

2 **tablespoons bourbon**

8 **lemon wedges**

8 **sprigs dill**

1. Rinse the salmon, pat dry and cut crosswise in half. Lay 1 piece skin side down
on the work surface. Sprinkle with half the herbs and peppercorns, all of the salt
and sugar, the bourbon, then the remaining herbs and peppercorns.

2. Place the second piece of salmon on top, skin side up, like a sandwich. Wrap
tightly in plastic wrap, place in a dish and refrigerate for 48 hours, turning every
8 hours. (If a lot of liquid accumulates in the dish, unwrap the salmon, baste with
the liquid and re-wrap.)

3. Remove the marinated salmon from the plastic and scrape away the herbs and
seasonings. Blot the salmon dry, then cut into paper-thin slices. Arrange on
chilled plates with a lemon wedge and dill sprig and serve with toast points.

Serves 8 as an appetizer

GREENBRIER QUICHE

We've transformed a classic quiche lorraine into our own favorite by adding some local Virginia ham and slices of savory oven-roasted tomato.

For the crust:

1 cup all-purpose flour

4 tablespoons cold unsalted butter, cut in pieces

1/2 teaspoon salt

1 egg yolk

1 - 3 tablespoons cold water

1/4 cup *diced Virginia ham*

1/2 cup minced onion (1/2 medium onion)

1 tablespoon unsalted butter

1/2 cup grated Asiago cheese (2 ounces)

1/2 cup grated Gruyere or Swiss cheese (2 ounces)

3 eggs

1 1/2 cups milk

1 tablespoon chopped fresh dill, or 1 teaspoon dried

Pinch freshly grated nutmeg

Salt and freshly ground black pepper, to taste

8 slices oven-roasted tomatoes (page 72)

8 medium sprigs dill

1. Make the crust: in a food processor, combine the flour, butter and salt and work with the pulse button until the mixture has the texture of coarse meal. With the motor running, add the yolk and just enough of the water for the dough to begin to form a loose ball. Transfer the dough to a lightly floured work surface and shape into a smooth ball. Cover the dough with plastic wrap and chill for at least 20 minutes.

2. Preheat the oven to 375F. Lightly butter a 10-inch quiche or tart pan. On a lightly floured work surface, roll out the dough to a circle approximately 15 inches in diameter and 1/8 inch thick. Lift the dough by rolling it loosely around the rolling pin and gently lay it in the pan, draping the dough in the pan as it is unrolled and pressing firmly into the corners. Trim off the excess crust and crimp the edges with your fingers or a fork for a decorative finish. **Blind-bake** the crust in the preheated oven until it is an even pale golden brown, about 15 minutes, then remove from the oven and cool slightly. Reduce the oven temperature to 350F.

3. In a small sauté pan, cook the ham and onion in the butter over medium heat until the onion is soft but not brown, about 4 minutes. Drain off any excess grease and sprinkle the onion, ham and cheeses evenly over the crust.

4. In a small bowl, whisk together the eggs and milk until well-blended, then add the chopped dill and season with nutmeg, salt and pepper (go easy on the salt, as the cheese and ham are salty). Pour the egg mixture into the crust. Place the tomato slices around the rim in an even pattern and arrange the dill sprigs in a decorative pattern in the center. Bake the quiche in the preheated oven until no longer liquid in the center, about 25 minutes. Remove and cool slightly before serving.

Makes 1 10-inch quiche

CILANTRO CREPES STUFFED WITH SHRIMP AND SHIITAKE MUSHROOMS

These crepes may be made ahead and frozen, to stuff at the last minute with this intriguing Asian-inspired filling.

For the crepes:

16 4-inch crepes
(page 74; see changes below)

1 tablespoon sesame oil

2 tablespoons finely chopped
fresh cilantro

1 medium bunch spring onions,
white part only, finely chopped

4 ounces shiitake mushrooms,
finely chopped (1½ cups)

1 tablespoon oil (such as canola,
soy or safflower)

2 medium cloves garlic, minced

8 ounces cooked, *peeled and deveined shrimp*, finely chopped

1 8-ounce can water chestnuts,
drained and finely chopped

Grated *zest* of 1 lime

⅓ cup *oyster sauce*

4 tablespoons chopped fresh
cilantro

½ teaspoon salt

¼ teaspoon crushed red pepper
flakes, or to taste

Good-quality soy sauce, for
dipping

1. Make the crepes as they appear in the recipe on page 74, except substitute the sesame oil for the melted butter and add the chopped cilantro; make them 4 inches in diameter, using about 1½ tablespoons batter per crepe. Separate the crepes with wax paper and reserve.

2. In a small sauté pan, cook the onions and mushrooms in the oil over medium-high heat until soft and just beginning to brown slightly, about 4 minutes. Add the garlic and continue to cook for another 30-60 seconds, then remove from the heat and cool.

3. Combine the cooled mushroom mixture with the cooked shrimp, water chestnuts, lime zest, oyster sauce, cilantro and salt and red pepper flakes. Taste and correct seasoning. Place 1 heaping tablespoon of the filling mixture on the center of each crepe. Fold up the bottom edge of the crepe, then the 2 sides, then roll the crepe into a neat cylindrical packet. Arrange the stuffed crepes, seam sides down, on a platter and serve chilled or at room temperature, with a small bowl of soy sauce for dipping.

Makes 16 crepes

Pictured above: Greenbrier Quiche, Cilantro Crepes Stuffed with Shrimp and Shiitake Mushrooms, Crabmeat Mayonnaise

CRABMEAT MAYONNAISE

A constant at Greenbrier receptions, this hors d'oeuvre features nuggets of sweet crabmeat cloaked in a creamy horseradish sauce.

1/2 cup mayonnaise

1/4 cup sour cream

2 teaspoons prepared horseradish, or freshly grated horseradish to taste

Juice of 1/2 lemon

1 pound cooked lump backfin crabmeat, picked over to remove any shell

Salt and freshly ground black pepper, to taste

Lemon slices

1. In a medium bowl, fold together the mayonnaise, sour cream, horseradish, lemon juice and crabmeat. Season to taste with salt and pepper. Chill for at least 1 hour before serving.

2. To serve, heap the crabmeat in a small chilled bowl, season with more freshly ground black pepper, decorate with lemon slices and serve with crackers or melba toast.

Serves 8 as an hors d'oeuvre

SPICED PECANS

The unusual combination of sweet and spicy makes these crunchy nuts irresistible.

8 tablespoons (1 stick) unsalted butter

1 1/2 cups brown sugar, packed

1 teaspoon dry mustard

1/2 teaspoon cayenne pepper

1 1/2 teaspoons ground cumin

1 egg white

1/2 pound shelled pecan halves

1. Preheat the oven to 300F. Melt the butter in a large skillet. Add the sugar and spices, remove from the heat and stir to dissolve. Let cool, then stir in the egg white. Pour the mixture over the pecans in a large bowl, then stir and toss until they are evenly coated.

2. Transfer the pecans to a baking sheet and spread them in a single layer. Toast in the preheated oven, shaking and tossing 2 - 3 times during cooking, until the pecans are golden brown, about 20 minutes altogether. Transfer the nuts to a bowl or tray. When the pecans are cool enough to handle, rub them between your hands to evenly distribute the sugar coating and avoid clumping. Cool completely. Serve as a snack or with cocktails.

Makes 1/2 pound

CARAMELIZED BRIE

What could be better than ripe runny Brie? How about ripe runny Brie with a topping of chewy caramel and crisp spiced nuts? Be careful if you serve this as an hors d'oeuvre — your guests might not save room for dinner!

²/₃ cup brown sugar, packed

¹/₃ cup water

¹/₂ cup heavy cream

4 tablespoons (¹/₂ stick) unsalted butter

¹/₂ cup Spiced Pecans (page 51) or plain pecan halves

1 ripe 8-inch wheel of Brie cheese, with top rind evenly cut off

1. Combine the brown sugar and water in a heavy-bottomed saucepan and bring to a boil. Cook over medium heat until the mixture reaches the soft ball stage (240F on a candy thermometer), about 4 minutes from the time the mixture begins to boil.

2. Let the mixture cool slightly, then stir in the cream. Continue to boil for another 3-4 minutes until the mixture is glossy and slightly thickened. Remove from the heat and stir in the butter. Fold in the spiced pecans.

3. Pour the caramel evenly over the top of the cheese so it coats the top surface and runs a little over the side, distributing the pecans with the help of a knife or spoon. Serve with slices of French bread, crackers or apple wedges.

Makes 1 8-inch round of cheese

Pictured at right: Caramelized Brie, Spiced Pecans, Greenbrier Buttermilk Biscuits

Soups & Salads

SEAFOOD GAZPACHO

*Garnish this refreshing soup with any combination of cooked seafood—even leftovers.
If fresh tomatoes aren't juicy and red, use good-quality canned ones instead.*

1 large red bell *pepper, cored,
seeded* and roughly chopped
(1¼ cups)

½ medium *cucumber, peeled,
seeded,* roughly chopped (1 cup)
(reserve the other half for
the garnish)

1 small rib celery, chopped
(⅓ cup)

1 small onion, chopped (¾ cup)

2 medium cloves garlic, minced

2 pounds *tomatoes, cored, seeded*
and roughly chopped (4 cups)

1 cup water

1 slice white bread, torn in
small pieces

¼ cup sherry vinegar or red
wine vinegar

¼ cup extra-virgin olive oil

1 teaspoon salt

Dash Tabasco sauce

For the garnish:

1 pound mixed cooked seafood
(such as crabmeat, shrimp,
scallops, mussels)

½ medium cucumber, peeled,
seeded and *diced* (1 cup)

1 small yellow or green bell
pepper, cored, seeded and diced
(¾ cup)

2 tablespoons fresh cilantro leaves

1. Combine all the ingredients, except the garnish ingredients, in a large bowl and marinate for at least 1 hour (be sure the bread is completely soaked). Puree the mixture in a blender until very smooth, then pass through a strainer into a bowl to remove any seeds or bits of skin. Chill thoroughly. Taste and correct seasoning.

2. To serve, ladle the chilled soup base into cold serving bowls, then garnish with the cooked seafood, diced vegetables and fresh cilantro.

Serves 8

THE GOLF CLUB VICHYSSOISE

A specialty of the Golf Club Buffet for many years.

2 tablespoons unsalted butter

3 cups thinly sliced *leek*
(3 medium leeks, white part only)

2 cups thinly sliced onion
(1 large onion)

4 cups *chicken stock,*
preferably homemade

1 1/2 cups *diced* potato
(8 ounces potato)

3 cups milk

Salt and freshly ground black
pepper, to taste

1 1/2 cups heavy cream, chilled

2 tablespoons minced fresh chives

1. Melt the butter in a large saucepan, add the leeks and onion and cook over low heat, stirring frequently, until they are very soft and translucent, 12-15 minutes.

2. Add the chicken stock and potatoes. **Simmer** the soup for another 30-35 minutes, covered, until the potatoes are very tender. Add the milk, bring the soup to a boil, then puree the soup in a blender (in batches if necessary). Season to taste with salt and pepper. Strain the soup through a fine-meshed strainer and chill thoroughly, at least 4 hours.

3. Just before serving, add the chilled cream to the soup; taste and correct seasoning. Ladle into chilled bowls, top with a pinch of fresh chives and serve.

Serves 8

GREENBRIER PEACH SOUP

Our famous peaches find their way into many dishes at The Greenbrier —
this easy-to-make chilled soup is one of the most popular.

2¹/₂ pounds *Greenbrier peaches*
(about 4 cups roughly chopped)
(reserve the juice)

1¹/₂ cups sour cream

¹/₂ cup pineapple juice

¹/₂ cup orange juice

¹/₄ cup lemon juice

¹/₄ cup dry sherry

1 cup reserved peach juice

8 mint sprigs

1. Combine the peaches and sour cream in a blender and work to a puree. Add the remaining ingredients (except the mint) and blend until very smooth.

2. Transfer to a bowl, cover and chill thoroughly, at least 2 hours, then ladle into chilled bowls, add the mint and serve.

Serves 8

BLACK BEAN SOUP

A favorite at Draper's Cafe, this satisfying soup can be a meal in itself.

1 cup chopped onion
(1 medium onion)

$^1/_3$ cup chopped celery
(1 medium rib celery)

$^1/_2$ cup chopped carrot
(1 medium carrot)

2 tablespoons unsalted butter

1 medium clove garlic, minced

$^1/_4$ cup *diced* ham

1$^1/_4$ cups (8 ounces) dried black
beans, rinsed and picked over

2 quarts *chicken stock,*
preferably homemade

1 bay leaf

1 sprig fresh thyme or
$^1/_4$ teaspoon dried

Salt and freshly ground black
pepper, to taste

$^1/_2$ cup sour cream

1 small red bell *pepper* (or a mix
of red, yellow and green bell
peppers), *cored, seeded* and finely
diced ($^3/_4$ cup)

1 tablespoon chopped fresh
parsley

1. In a large saucepan, cook the onion, celery and carrot in the butter over medium heat until soft but not brown, about 5 minutes. Add the garlic and ham and cook for 2 more minutes.

2. Add the beans, chicken stock, bay leaf and thyme. Bring to a boil, reduce the heat, cover and cook until the beans are very tender, about 2 hours. Season to taste with salt and pepper.

3. Remove the bay leaf and thyme sprig, then puree the cooked beans and their liquid in a blender until very smooth. (Puree the soup in batches if necessary.) Taste and correct seasoning. To serve, ladle the hot soup into warmed bowls. Top with a tablespoon of sour cream, then sprinkle with diced peppers and parsley.

Serves 8

FIVE-ONION SOUP WITH CRISPY SHALLOTS AND FRESH CHIVES

Patience in slowly cooking the onions until they are a deep caramel brown will be rewarded by the heady flavor of this elegant soup, created by our Tavern Room chefs.

2 tablespoons unsalted butter

4 medium shallots (4 ounces), roughly chopped

1 medium *leek,* white part only (4 ounces), roughly chopped

1 medium red onion (8 ounces), roughly chopped

2 medium yellow onions (1 pound), roughly chopped

1 bunch green onions, white part only, roughly chopped

2 quarts *chicken stock,* preferably homemade

1½ cups heavy cream

Salt and freshly ground black pepper, to taste

For the garnish:

2 shallots, cut in half lengthwise and sliced as thinly as possible

1 teaspoon all-purpose flour

Oil (such as canola, soy or safflower), for deep-frying

1 tablespoon minced fresh chives

1. In a large heavy-bottomed saucepan, melt the butter and add the shallots, leek and all the onions. Cover and cook over low heat, stirring frequently to prevent burning, until the onions are soft and have turned deep golden brown, 20-30 minutes.

2. Add the chicken stock and *simmer* uncovered until the onions are very soft, about another 20 minutes.

3. Transfer the soup to a blender and blend until very smooth (do this in batches if necessary). Return the soup to a clean pan, add the cream and bring to a boil. (Simmer the soup a few minutes to thicken slightly, if necessary.) Season with salt and pepper to taste.

4. To make the shallot garnish: sprinkle the sliced shallots with the flour, then toss in a fine strainer to thoroughly coat the shallots and shake off excess flour. Fill a saucepan no more than ⅓ full with oil. Heat the oil to 375F (if not using a thermometer, fry a few test pieces first.) Carefully drop the shallots in the oil and fry, stirring to prevent sticking. The shallots should cook slowly, getting light brown after about 45 seconds. When golden brown (no darker than a brown paper bag) remove from the oil with a slotted spoon and drain on paper towels. The garnish may be made up to 8 hours ahead and stored in an airtight container. To serve, ladle the hot soup into warm bowls and top with a spoonful of crispy shallots and a pinch of fresh chives.

Serves 8

CREAM OF RED BELL PEPPER SOUP

A stunning scarlet soup with the mellow flavor of roasted peppers—excellent as a chilled soup, too.

6 medium red bell peppers
(2½ pounds)

1½ cups *diced* onion
(1 large onion)

½ cup diced carrot
(1 medium carrot)

2 tablespoons unsalted butter

2 cloves garlic, minced

1 cup dry white wine

6 cups *chicken stock,* preferably
homemade

1 bay leaf

Salt and cayenne pepper, to taste

2 cups heavy cream

1 tablespoon chopped mixed fresh
herbs (such as parsley, chives,
chervil, basil)

1. Preheat the broiler. Place the peppers on a baking sheet and broil close to the heat, turning the peppers as necessary until charred and blistered on all surfaces. Transfer them to a plastic bag and leave until cool enough to handle, at least 10 minutes. (The steam created in the bag will enable the skins to slip off easily.) Peel off all the skin, remove and discard the core and all the seeds. Cut the peppers into rough dice. (The peppers may be prepared up to 1 day ahead.)

2. In a large pot, cook the onion and carrot in the butter until soft but not brown, about 5 minutes. Add the garlic and continue cooking another 1-2 minutes, then add the peppers and white wine. Bring to a boil and cook until the wine is *reduced* by half. Add the chicken stock and bay leaf and season to taste with salt and pepper. Leave to *simmer* until all the vegetables are very soft, about 20 minutes.

3. Remove the bay leaf and puree the soup in a blender or food processor. Pass through a sieve to remove any bits of skin and seeds and return the soup to a clean pan. Add the cream, bring to a boil and boil for 2-3 minutes. Taste and correct seasoning. Serve hot or cold, with a pinch of chopped herbs to decorate.

Serves 8

NEWPORT CRABMEAT AND LOBSTER CHOWDER

Saffron adds a fragrant dimension to this seafood soup. Shrimp, scallops and chunks of white fish would be appropriate substitutes for the crab and lobster, too.

3 tablespoons unsalted butter

1 1/2 cups *diced* red pepper
(1 large red pepper)

1 cup diced onion
(1 medium onion)

1 cup diced celery
(3 medium ribs celery)

2 quarts *fish stock*
(or 4 cups bottled clam juice
and 4 cups water)

8 ounces new potatoes, diced
(1 1/2 cups)

Pinch saffron threads

2 sprigs fresh thyme, or
1/2 teaspoon dried

3/4 cup cooked lobster meat,
cut in small chunks

3/4 cup cooked lump crabmeat,
picked over to remove any
shell and flaked

Salt and freshly ground black
pepper, to taste

1. In a large saucepan, melt the butter and cook the pepper, onion and celery over medium heat, stirring frequently, until the vegetables are soft and translucent, 4-6 minutes.

2. Add the fish stock, potatoes, saffron and thyme and *simmer* the soup until the potatoes are tender, 25-30 minutes. Remove the thyme sprigs and discard. Add the lobster and crab; simmer for 2-3 more minutes to heat the seafood. Season to taste with salt and pepper. Ladle into warmed bowls and serve hot.

Serves 8

GREENBRIER TWO-BEAN CHILI
WITH CILANTRO CREAM

*A spoonful of the cilantro cream will temper the heat in this zesty chili.
Use the best quality chili powder available — we use Hatch's from Sante Fe.*

1 small bunch fresh cilantro,
leaves picked and stems discarded

1 cup crème fraîche or sour cream

Salt and freshly ground black
pepper, to taste

3 tablespoons extra-virgin
olive oil

2 pounds lean ground beef

1 cup chopped onion
(1 medium onion)

3 tablespoons good quality
chili powder

2 teaspoons ground cumin

3 cups drained chopped
canned tomatoes

1¹/2 cups *chicken or veal stock*

6 tablespoons tomato paste

2¹/2 cups cooked and drained
kidney beans (1 26-ounce can)

1¹/2 cups cooked and drained
black beans (1 15-ounce can)

Salt and Tabasco sauce, to taste

1. **Blanch** the cilantro leaves, drain and rinse immediately under very cold water, then dry on paper towels. Combine the cilantro and a few spoons of the crème fraîche in a blender or food processor and process until the herbs are finely chopped, then stir into the remaining cream and season to taste with salt and pepper.

2. In a large sauté pan, heat 1 tablespoon of the oil and cook the ground beef gently over medium heat until it is no longer pink (do not overcook). Transfer the meat to a strainer or colander and drain thoroughly.

3. In a large pot, heat the remaining oil and cook the onion over medium heat until soft but not brown, about 4 minutes. Stir in the chili powder and cumin and cook for 30-60 seconds, then add the drained meat, tomatoes, stock and tomato paste. **Simmer** over low heat to combine the flavors and thicken the chili slightly, about 15 minutes. Add both kinds of bean and continue to simmer another 5-10 minutes. Season to taste with salt and Tabasco sauce. Serve hot with a dollop of cilantro cream.

Serves 8 as a first course

Greenbrier Salads

At The Greenbrier, we serve hundreds of salads of all types, but our signature salad consists of a theme with unlimited variations. We choose the freshest young greens and combine them into satisfying blends of taste, texture and color — perhaps some tender red oak leaf lettuce with bitter frisee, or buttery Bibb and peppery watercress.

The greens serve as a backdrop for a complementary garnish, such as our pungent oven-roasted tomatoes, crisp and delicate Stilton-Saga lace crackers or creamy slices of West Virginia chevre cheese rolled in crisp nuts.

The diner always has a choice of dressings. Most popular is our house dressing, tangy with whole-grained mustard, and we're proud of our new Greenbrier Light dressing, which is low in fat but high in flavor.

The following pages contain recipes for our favorite dressings and salad garnishes. Be creative and prepare your own distinctive and delicious combinations, to serve at the beginning of a meal or even after the main course, as we do in our more formal dinners.

MUSTARD VINAIGRETTE— OUR HOUSE DRESSING

This is our most popular dressing—we even sell it in our Gourmet Shop.
Not just for salads, it works as a dip for raw vegetables or drizzled
over fresh steamed asparagus.

1 egg yolk

¹/₂ cup white wine vinegar or
cider vinegar

1 tablespoon whole-grained
mustard

1 tablespoon lemon juice

2 teaspoons granulated sugar

1 teaspoon Worcestershire sauce

1 teaspoon salt

¹/₄ teaspoon white pepper

1 cup oil (such as canola,
safflower or soy)

1. In a medium bowl, whisk together all the ingredients except the oil.

2. Add the oil in a slow steady drizzle, whisking constantly until emulsified with the other ingredients. Taste and correct seasoning. (The dressing may be stored in the refrigerator 3-4 days.)

Makes 1¹/₂ cups

"GREENBRIER LIGHT" HERBAL DRESSING

Developed for our "Greenbrier Light" program, this dressing has all the zest
of a traditional vinaigrette with just a fraction of the oil.

1 cup *chicken stock,* preferably
homemade, all fat removed

1 tablespoon *arrowroot,* dissolved
in 1 tablespoon cold water

3 tablespoons red wine vinegar

1 teaspoon lemon juice

1 teaspoon dry mustard

1 teaspoon granulated sugar

½ clove garlic, minced

4 teaspoons extra-virgin olive oil

1 tablespoon mixed chopped fresh
herbs (such as cilantro, chives,
basil, parsley)

Salt and freshly ground black
pepper, to taste

1. Bring the chicken stock to a boil in a small saucepan and whisk in the dissolved arrowroot until thickened. Leave to cool.

2. Combine the vinegar, lemon juice, mustard, sugar and garlic in a small bowl, whisking until the mustard and sugar are dissolved. Whisk the thickened chicken stock into the mixture, then whisk in the olive oil, bit by bit. Add the herbs and season to taste with salt and pepper. (The dressing will get very thick when refrigerated, so leave at room temperature 1 hour before serving; it may be refrigerated up to 1 week.)

Makes 1¼ cups

TAVERN CAESAR DRESSING

A bold dressing to toss with hearts of romaine lettuce and croutons for a classic Caesar salad.

1 egg yolk

2 tablespoons lemon juice

2 tablespoons white wine

1 teaspoon Worcestershire sauce

6 anchovy filets, drained and
roughly chopped

2 cloves garlic, roughly chopped

1/2 teaspoon freshly ground black
pepper

1 cup extra-virgin olive oil

3 tablespoons freshly grated
Parmesan cheese

1 teaspoon chopped fresh parsley

1. Place the egg yolk, lemon juice, wine, Worcestershire sauce, anchovies, garlic and pepper in a food processor and process until smooth.

2. With the motor running, add the olive oil in a thin stream and process until the dressing is creamy and emulsified. Add the cheese and parsley and process a few more seconds. Taste and correct seasoning. (The dressing may be mixed with a hand whisk instead of the processor but the consistency will be less creamy. If mixing by hand, be sure to finely chop the anchovies and garlic before adding.)

Makes 1 1/2 cups

STILTON-SAGA LACE CRACKERS

These crisp and delicate crackers add an intense cheesy accent to a green salad.
We use a blend of blue cheeses, but a single cheese with a not-too-creamy texture will work well also.

**4 ounces Stilton cheese,
rind removed**

**4 ounces Saga cheese,
rind removed**

**8 tablespoons (1 stick) unsalted
butter, slightly softened at
room temperature**

1/2 cup all-purpose flour

1. Preheat the oven to 400F. With an electric mixer, or by hand with a wooden spoon, cream together the cheeses and the butter until fairly smooth. Add the flour and mix until just barely incorporated.

2. Lay a large piece of plastic wrap on the work surface and spoon the dough into a log shape along a short end. Using the plastic, shape the log into an even cylinder 1 1/2 inches in diameter. Wrap tightly in the plastic and refrigerate until firm, at least 2 hours. (The dough may be prepared up to 2 days ahead.)

3. When the dough is firm, unwrap the plastic and, with a sharp knife, cut into 1/8-inch rounds (don't worry if the slices are not perfectly even, as they will spread during cooking anyway). Place the rounds on a baking sheet at least 2 inches apart. Bake in the preheated oven until the crackers are very lacy and golden brown through the center, about 8 minutes. Remove the baking sheet from the oven and cool for a couple of minutes before lifting the crackers from the sheet with a thin spatula. (They are very fragile, especially when hot, so allow a few extras for breakage.) Serve at room temperature on a green salad.

Makes approximately 3 dozen

Pictured at left: Stilton-Saga Lace Crackers, Oven-Roasted Tomatoes

OVEN-ROASTED TOMATOES

There are no trick techniques needed for this recipe—just time! The results are intensely flavored slices of tomato, to enliven a salad, garnish an omelet or feature as part of an antipasto platter.

6 large plum tomatoes, cored and sliced lengthwise into 3/8-inch slices

2 tablespoons extra-virgin olive oil

1 clove garlic, minced

2 teaspoons minced shallot

2 teaspoons chopped fresh basil or 1/2 teaspoon dried

1 teaspoon chopped fresh oregano or 1/4 teaspoon dried

1/2 teaspoon chopped fresh thyme or 1/8 teaspoon dried

1/2 teaspoon freshly ground black pepper

1/8 teaspoon salt

1. Preheat the oven to 250F. Toss all the ingredients together until the tomato slices are evenly coated. Lay the tomatoes on a wire rack and position the rack on a baking sheet to catch the drips.

2. Roast the tomatoes in the warm oven until they have lost much of their moisture and are slightly leathery in appearance, about 2 hours. Remove from the oven and leave on the rack to cool. Serve slightly chilled or at room temperature. (The tomatoes may be stored in the refrigerator up to 4 days.)

Makes about 1 1/2 dozen slices

CHEVRE IN PHYLLO PASTRY

Layers of flaky phyllo pastry contain a creamy center, the perfect enhancement to a salad of tender mixed greens.

8 ounces fresh *chevre* cheese, preferably log-shaped

Salt and freshly ground black pepper, to taste

2 tablespoons mixed chopped fresh herbs (such as parsley, dill, basil, tarragon, chervil) or 2 teaspoons dried

3 sheets *phyllo dough*

3 tablespoons unsalted butter, melted

1/4 cup lightly toasted bread crumbs

2 6-inch crepes (see recipe below)

1. Preheat the oven to 400F. Blot the chevre with paper towels to remove any excess moisture and split it lengthwise to create 2 long thin pieces, rolling gently if necessary to reshape them into neat cylinders. Season the cheese with salt and pepper, then roll in the chopped herbs to coat.

2. Lay out 1 sheet of phyllo on the work surface, with the long sides running vertically. Brush the entire surface with melted butter, then sprinkle with 1/3 of the crumbs. Cover the first sheet with a second sheet and repeat with butter and crumbs. Repeat with a third sheet of phyllo, butter and the remaining crumbs. Place 2 crepes across the closest short side and lay the 2 pieces of cheese end-to-end on the crepes, squeezing slightly to join them into 1 long log. Roll the crepes and phyllo sheets tightly around the cheese and continue rolling, tucking in the ends, until the phyllo is all wrapped around the cheese. Place the roll, seam side down, on a baking sheet and brush the entire surface with more melted butter.

3. Bake in the preheated oven until golden brown, 25 - 30 minutes. Remove from the oven and cool for 15 minutes before slicing (for best results, use a serrated knife). Serve warm on a green salad, or as a first course.

Serves 8

Crepes

This recipe makes more than needed for the chevre in phyllo, but as they freeze beautifully, keep the extras on hand in the freezer for a quick dessert or luncheon dish, or to make the cilantro crepe appetizer on page 49.

3/4 cup all-purpose flour

Pinch salt

2 eggs

1 cup milk

2 tablespoons unsalted butter, melted

Clarified butter or oil, for frying

1. Place the flour and salt in a small bowl and make a well in the center. Add the eggs to the well and whisk to mix the eggs. Continue whisking in small circles, drawing in a little flour at a time. Add the milk gradually, still whisking in the center, incorporating the flour slowly until all the flour is mixed and the batter is smooth. Add the melted butter and whisk again. Let the batter rest about 15 minutes, then add a little more milk if necessary to get the consistency of heavy cream.

2. Heat a small non-stick crepe pan (or frying pan with curved sides) and brush the surface with a little butter or oil. Pour in a small amount of batter, about 2 tablespoons, and quickly tilt and shake the pan until the batter covers the surface of the pan in a smooth layer. Gently fry 1 - 2 minutes, then flip the crepe and fry the other side. Transfer the finished crepe to a plate. The crepes may be stored in the refrigerator 2 - 3 days or frozen up to 3 months. (To prevent their sticking together, separate each crepe with a piece of wax paper.)

Makes about 15 6-inch crepes

Pictured at right: Chevre in Phyllo Pastry, Wild Mushroom Strudel

WILD MUSHROOM STRUDEL

A slice of this strudel brings the earthy flavor of mushrooms and the crunch of phyllo pastry to a fresh green salad. It's a nice idea for a first course, too.

2 cups chopped mixed fresh *wild mushrooms* (choose from chanterelles, shiitakes, morels) (6 ounces)

2 cups chopped common mushrooms (6 ounces)

5 tablespoons unsalted butter

2 medium shallots (2 ounces), chopped

Salt and freshly ground black pepper, to taste

2 tablespoons chopped mixed fresh herbs (such as parsley, basil, dill, tarragon, chervil) or 2 teaspoons dried

1 egg, lightly beaten

3 sheets *phyllo dough*

1/4 cup lightly toasted bread crumbs

2 6-inch crepes (page 74)

1. In a large sauté pan, *sauté* all the mushrooms in 2 tablespoons of the butter over medium-high heat until all their liquid has been rendered and evaporated and the mushrooms are golden and crisp, 8 - 10 minutes. Add the shallots, season with salt and pepper and continue cooking 2 more minutes. Remove from the heat and stir in the herbs. Taste and correct seasoning, then chill the mixture. When the mushrooms are cool, stir in the beaten egg. (The mushroom mixture may be prepared up to 1 day ahead, however DO NOT add the egg until the last minute.)

2. Preheat the oven to 400F. Melt the remaining butter. Lay out 1 sheet of phyllo on the work surface, with the long sides running vertically. Brush the entire surface with melted butter, then sprinkle with 1/3 of the crumbs. Cover the first sheet with a second sheet and repeat with butter and crumbs. Repeat with a third sheet of phyllo, butter and the remaining crumbs. Place 2 crepes across the closest short side and mound the chilled mushroom mixture in a line across the crepes, leaving a 1 1/2-inch margin at either end. Pat the mushrooms into a neat cylinder, fold the margins in, then roll the crepes and phyllo sheets around the filling and continue rolling until all the pastry is wrapped around the filling. Place the roll, seam side down, on a baking sheet and brush the entire surface with more melted butter.

3. Bake in the preheated oven until golden brown, 25 - 30 minutes. Remove from the oven and cool for 15 minutes before slicing (for best results, use a serrated knife). Serve warm on a green salad or as a first course.

Serves 8

NUT-CRUSTED CHEVRE

Crunchy vs. creamy is the dynamic in this savory salad garnish. Try rolling the cheese into bite-sized balls for canapes, too.

1/4 cup (2 ounces) pecan halves
or pieces

1/4 cup (2 ounces) macadamia nuts

1/4 cup (2 ounces) skinless
hazelnuts

8 ounces fresh *chevre* cheese,
preferably log-shaped

Salt and freshly ground black
pepper, to taste

1 egg, lightly beaten

Oil (such as canola, soy or
safflower), for frying

1. Preheat the oven to 400F. Lightly toast all the nuts by laying them on a baking sheet and roasting in the preheated oven until slightly darker in color and very fragrant, 5 - 6 minutes. Leave to cool, then chop them finely in a food processor, using the pulse button to prevent the nuts from being overworked into a powder or paste. (Alternatively, chop the nuts finely with a knife.) Transfer the chopped nuts to a plate.

2. Blot the chevre with paper towels to remove any excess moisture. (If the log is flattened on 1 side, gently roll the cheese to reshape in a neat cylinder.) Cut the cheese into 8 even rounds. Season the rounds with salt and pepper, dip in the beaten egg, then dip in the chopped nuts to coat thoroughly. Let the coated rounds dry for a few minutes before frying.

3. Add just enough oil to a non-stick frying pan to coat the bottom. When the oil is hot, add the cheese rounds and fry gently until golden brown, about 2 minutes on each side. Drain on paper towels and serve warm with a green salad.

Serves 8

Fish & Shellfish

SALMON AND STURGEON SCALLOPINI IN CAVIAR BUTTER SAUCE

The subtle richness of the flavors and the delicate peach and ivory hues make this a truly elegant dish, perfect for the poshest of parties.

3/4 cup heavy cream

1 cup dry white wine

1/4 cup white wine vinegar

6 stems parsley

10 whole black peppercorns

2 medium shallots, minced

18 tablespoons (2 sticks plus 2 tablespoons) unsalted butter, cut into small pieces

Salt and white pepper, to taste

1 1/4 pounds salmon filet, cut into 8 1/4-inch slices

1 1/4 pounds sturgeon filet (or other white fish such as sole), cut into 8 1/4-inch slices

2 tablespoons caviar or other fish roe

1 tablespoon minced fresh chives

1. Make the sauce: in a heavy saucepan, boil the cream until it is *reduced* to 1/3 cup. In a separate saucepan, combine the wine, vinegar, parsley stems, peppercorns and shallots and boil until the liquid is very syrupy and reduced to 1 tablespoon.

2. Add the reduced cream to the wine reduction, remove the pan from the heat and whisk in 16 tablespoons of the butter bit by bit until it is well-incorporated and the sauce is emulsified. Strain the sauce, then season to taste with salt and white pepper. Keep warm in a *water bath.*

3. Season the fish with salt and white pepper. Heat the remaining butter in a large sauté pan and quickly *sauté* the fish until just barely opaque in the center, about 1 minute on each side. Arrange 1 piece of salmon and 1 piece of sturgeon on each warmed plate, or on a platter. Pour a ribbon of butter sauce around the fish and sprinkle on some caviar. Finish with a pinch of chives and serve immediately.

Serves 8

BROILED SNAPPER WITH SAFFRON SHALLOT VINAIGRETTE

An unusual treatment for a main dish, this warm saffron vinaigrette gives an assertive accent to the mild snapper filet.

8 6-ounce skinless
snapper filets

Salt and freshly ground black
pepper, to taste

4 tablespoons chopped mixed
fresh herbs (choose from basil,
dill, chervil, parsley)

3/4 cup extra-virgin olive oil

2 medium shallots
(2 ounces), minced

1/2 cup rice wine vinegar

1 pinch saffron threads

1 large *tomato, peeled, seeded* and
cut into small *dice* (1 cup)

1. Preheat the broiler. Season both sides of the filets with salt and pepper and half of the chopped herbs. Drizzle with 3 tablespoons of the olive oil and marinate in the refrigerator while making the sauce.

2. Combine the shallots, vinegar and saffron in a small saucepan and boil until the volume is *reduced* by half. Add the diced tomato and *simmer* to heat through, 1-2 minutes.

3. With the mixture boiling gently, whisk in the remaining olive oil, bit by bit to emulsify. Add the remaining herbs, and season to taste with salt and pepper. Keep warm. (The emulsion of oil and vinegar may separate; simply whisk together again just before serving.)

4. Arrange the marinated fish on a broiler rack and broil 2 inches from the heat until just barely opaque in the center, 2 - 3 minutes on each side for a 3/4-inch filet. Transfer the filets to warmed serving dishes or a platter and spoon on a little of the warm vinaigrette. Pass the rest separately.

Serves 8

HERB-CRUSTED GROUPER FILETS

This flavor-packed herb crust helps keep the filets moist.
Use it on other varieties of fish, too, such as salmon or snapper.

2 medium cloves garlic, minced

1/3 cup extra-virgin olive oil

8 6-ounce grouper filets

Salt and freshly ground black
pepper, to taste

1 cup fresh bread crumbs

1 cup roughly chopped mixed
fresh herbs (such as chives,
cilantro, basil, dill and parsley)

2 medium shallots (2 ounces),
minced

1 teaspoon grated fresh ginger

4 tablespoons unsalted butter,
melted

1. Combine the garlic and oil, brush evenly onto the grouper filets and season
with salt and pepper. Cover and marinate in the refrigerator 30-60 minutes.

2. Preheat the oven to 425F. In a small bowl, combine the bread crumbs, herbs,
shallots, ginger and butter and season to taste with salt and pepper. Scrape any
excess marinade from the filets and press 1/8 of the herb mixture (about 2
tablespoons) onto 1 side of each filet. Arrange on a baking sheet or roasting pan
and cook in the preheated oven until the crumbs are lightly browned and the fish
is just opaque in the center, about 15 minutes for a 3/4-inch filet. Arrange on
warmed plates or a platter and serve immediately.

Serves 8

ALLEGHENY MOUNTAIN TROUT
WITH SWEET POTATO, APPLE AND ONION HASH

*This combination of fresh trout and crispy hash makes an ideal breakfast
for an active day of skiing, hiking or hunting.*

8 10-ounce whole boneless trout,
or 2½ pounds of trout filets

¼ cup extra-virgin olive oil

Salt and freshly ground black
pepper, to taste

1 tablespoon chopped fresh thyme
or 1 teaspoon dried

4 strips bacon, *diced*

4 tablespoons unsalted butter

4 cups finely diced sweet potato
(1½ pounds)

1½ cups finely chopped onion
(1 large onion)

3 tart apples, peeled, cored and
cut into ¼-inch dice

1. Rinse the fish and pat dry with paper towels. Brush them, inside and out, with the oil and sprinkle with salt and pepper and 2 teaspoons of the thyme. Cover and marinate in the refrigerator for 30 minutes.

2. In a large sauté pan, cook the diced bacon until brown and crisp. Remove with a slotted spoon, leaving the fat in the pan, and drain on paper towels. Add the butter to the bacon fat, then add the diced sweet potato and *sauté* over medium heat, turning frequently, until the potato is slightly tender and light brown, about 15 minutes. Add the onion and continue to sauté another 5 minutes, then add the apple and cook until all the ingredients are tender and the hash is golden and crispy, another 4-5 minutes. Add the remaining thyme, the cooked bacon, and season generously with salt and pepper. Keep warm.

3. Preheat the broiler. Arrange the marinated fish on a rack or roasting pan and broil 2 inches from the heat until just barely opaque in the center, 2 - 3 minutes on each side for a whole fish and 1 - 2 minutes for a filet. To serve, arrange the hash on a warmed platter or plates and place the broiled trout on top. Serve immediately.

Serves 8

Pictured at left: Allegheny Mountain Trout with Sweet Potato, Apple and Onion Hash

BROILED SALMON WITH LENTIL RAGOUT AND HORSERADISH CREAM

The savory lentil ragout gives this dish an appealing earthiness, with a lively bite of horseradish. The recipe is adapted from our "Greenbrier Light" program, so fat is kept to a minimum.

1/2 cup plain low-fat yogurt

1/2 cup sour cream

1/2 cup grated peeled Granny Smith or other tart apple

1 tablespoon prepared horseradish or 2 teaspoons freshly grated

Salt and freshly ground black pepper, to taste

2 slices (about 1 ounce) bacon, cut crosswise into thin strips

3/4 cup finely *diced leek* (1 medium leek, white part only)

1/2 cup finely diced carrot (1 medium carrot)

1/4 cup finely diced celery (1 small rib celery)

6 tablespoons minced shallot (2 medium shallots)

3 medium cloves garlic, minced

1/4 cup dry white wine

1 sprig fresh thyme or 1/4 teaspoon dried

1 bay leaf

1 cup (6 ounces) green lentils

2 cups *chicken stock,* preferably homemade

2 tablespoons lime juice

2 tablespoons extra-virgin olive oil

2 1/2 pounds salmon filets

8 thin slices Granny Smith apple, peel on, rubbed with lemon to prevent browning

1 tablespoon chopped fresh parsley or chives

1. Put the yogurt in a coffee filter and drain in a strainer for 2 hours, or until reduced in volume by half. (This step is optional but it will make the sauce thicker and creamier.) Combine the drained yogurt with the sour cream, grated apple, horseradish and season to taste with salt and pepper. (The horseradish cream may be made up to 1 day ahead.)

2. In a large sauté pan or skillet, cook the bacon over medium heat until it is crisp and brown and has rendered its fat, 2-3 minutes. Add the leeks, carrots, and celery and cook until soft but not brown, stirring frequently, about 5 minutes. Add the shallots, a third of the garlic, white wine, thyme and bay leaf. Cook a few more minutes until the wine has evaporated.

3. Add the lentils and chicken stock, reduce the heat, cover and cook until the lentils are very tender and almost all the liquid is absorbed, about 35 minutes. (Add a little more stock or water if the lentils get too dry during cooking.) Season to taste with salt and pepper. Remove and discard the thyme sprig and the bay leaf. Keep warm. (The lentil ragout may be made up to 1 day ahead.)

4. Preheat the broiler. Combine the lime juice, olive oil and remaining garlic and brush on the fish. Season with salt and pepper. Broil 2 inches from the heat until just cooked through, 2 - 3 minutes on each side for a $1/2$-inch filet. To serve, arrange a bed of lentil ragout on warmed plates or a platter and place the broiled fish on top. Top with some horseradish cream and decorate with an apple slice and a pinch of chopped parsley and serve immediately.

Serves 8

POACHED BLACK BASS WITH
RED PEPPER COULIS

At The Greenbrier, we know that elegant meals and healthful dining are not mutually exclusive.
Adapted from our "Greenbrier Light" repertoire, this dish has no added fat,
yet is brimming with flavor and makes a stunning statement on the plate.

**4 medium red bell peppers
(1¹/₂ pounds)**

**2 medium shallots (2 ounces),
minced**

2 cups dry white wine

**4 cups *fish stock* (or 2 cups bottled
clam juice and 2 cups water) or
chicken stock, preferably
homemade**

**Salt and freshly ground black
pepper, to taste**

Lemon juice, to taste

8 6-ounce black bass filets

1. Preheat the broiler. Place the peppers on a baking sheet and roast close to the heat until charred and blistered on all surfaces, turning the peppers as necessary. Transfer them to a plastic bag and leave until cool enough to handle, at least 10 minutes. (The steam created in the bag will enable the skins to slip off easily.) Peel off all the skin, remove and discard the core and all the seeds. Cut the peppers into rough *dice.*

2. In a medium heavy-bottomed saucepan, combine the shallots and 1 cup of the wine and boil until *reduced* to 1 tablespoon of syrupy liquid. Add 3 cups of the stock and *simmer* until reduced by half. Add the diced red peppers, season with salt and pepper and simmer until the peppers are very soft, another 5-7 minutes.

3. Process the pepper mixture in a blender or food processor until very smooth and pourable. Add a few drops lemon juice, then taste and correct seasoning. (If the *coulis* seems too thick, dilute with a little stock.) Strain the coulis through a fine sieve to remove any bits of skin or seeds. (The coulis may be prepared up to 1 day ahead and reheated.)

4. Preheat the oven to 400F. Heat the remaining wine and stock, which will serve as the poaching liquid, in a small saucepan until simmering. Season the bass filets on both sides with salt and pepper. Lay them in a single layer in a shallow oven-proof dish or skillet. Pour on enough of the poaching liquid to just barely cover the filets, adding a little hot water if necessary. Cover the pan with aluminum foil or a lid and *poach* in the preheated oven until the filets are just opaque in the center, 7 - 8 minutes. Remove from the oven. Lift the filets from the poaching liquid with a slotted spatula, drain briefly on a paper towel, then arrange on warmed plates or a platter. Pour a ribbon of the coulis around the fish, and pass the remaining coulis separately.

Serves 8

KATE'S MOUNTAIN BARBECUED SHRIMP WITH SPICY REMOULADE SAUCE

Don't be intimidated by the long list of ingredients—the recipe is very quick and easy.
Hot or cold, these spicy shrimp are fabulous for a casual dinner or even as an hors d'oeuvre.

For the remoulade sauce:

1/2 cup mayonnaise

1/4 cup finely *diced* celery

2 tablespoons finely chopped green onions

2 tablespoons finely chopped fresh parsley

2 tablespoons prepared mustard

2 tablespoons prepared horseradish

2 tablespoons ketchup

2 teaspoons lemon juice

2 teaspoons white wine vinegar

1 teaspoon Worcestershire sauce

Few drops Tabasco sauce

1/2 teaspoon finely minced garlic

1/2 teaspoon salt

1/4 teaspoon dry mustard

1/4 teaspoon paprika

1 anchovy filet, drained and finely chopped

For the spice mixture:

1 tablespoon mild chili powder

1 teaspoon ground cumin

1 teaspoon granulated sugar

1 teaspoon salt

1/2 teaspoon dry mustard

1/2 teaspoon dried thyme

1/2 teaspoon freshly ground black pepper

1/2 teaspoon curry powder

1/4 teaspoon cayenne pepper

2 tablespoons extra-virgin olive oil

2 1/2 pounds large *shrimp* (about 20 per pound), *peeled and deveined*

Olive oil, for brushing the grill or skillet

1. Make the sauce: mix all the ingredients together in a bowl, pressing with a spoon to mash the onion, garlic and anchovy. Cover with plastic wrap and chill for at least 1 hour (the flavor will be better after 24 hours).

2. Pat the shrimp dry with paper towels. Combine all the ingredients in the spice mixture together in a large bowl. Add the shrimp and toss until evenly coated. Cover and marinate in the refrigerator 30 minutes.

3. Heat a grill or a heavy skillet. Brush it with a little olive oil and grill the shrimp until just barely opaque in the center, 1-2 minutes on each side. Arrange on a warmed platter or plates and serve the remoulade sauce in a cup for dipping. The shrimp are also good cold.

Serves 8

WARM SHRIMP SALAD WITH CALAMATA OLIVES AND BASIL

The Mediterranean flavors of this entree salad suit a hot summer night beautifully.
The vegetables should be just "flashed" through the pan to keep them slightly crunchy.

1/2 cup rice wine vinegar

2 tablespoons lemon juice

2 cloves garlic, minced

Salt and freshly ground black pepper, to taste

1 1/2 cups plus 2 tablespoons extra-virgin olive oil

2 1/2 pounds tiger prawns (13-15 per pound), or other large raw *shrimp, peeled and deveined*

1 small eggplant (12 ounces), peeled, cut into 1/2-inch *dice* and *degorged*

2 medium *tomatoes* (1 pound), *peeled, seeded* and cut into large dice

2 medium shallots (2 ounces), chopped

1/4 cup pitted good-quality black olives (such as Calamata), quartered

4 tablespoons *chiffonade* of fresh basil

1 pound mixed greens (such as Bibb, romaine, frisee, oak leaf, mache, arugula), torn into pieces

1 ounce feta cheese, crumbled

1. In a small bowl combine the vinegar, lemon juice, garlic, salt and pepper. Add 1 1/2 cups of the oil bit by bit, whisking constantly to emulsify. Taste and correct seasoning. Pour half of the vinaigrette over the raw shrimp and toss to coat. Cover and marinate in the refrigerator 2-3 hours. Reserve the remaining vinaigrette.

2. Blot the moisture from the eggplant with a paper towel. In a large sauté pan, heat the remaining 2 tablespoons of oil until very hot and *sauté* the eggplant until golden brown on all sides, about 3 minutes, shaking the pan to prevent sticking. Add the tomatoes and shallots and sauté another minute then remove from the heat and add the chopped olives and the basil. Season to taste with salt and pepper. Keep warm.

3. Drain the shrimp thoroughly and discard the marinade. Heat a large non-stick sauté pan and sauté the shrimp over high heat until just barely opaque in the center, about 2 minutes on each side (do this in batches if necessary to avoid crowding the pan). To serve, arrange a bed of greens on one half of a serving platter or individual plates. Mound the warm vegetables on the other half and arrange the sautéed shrimp in a row down the center. Drizzle on the reserved vinaigrette and sprinkle the feta cheese on top. Serve warm.

Serves 8

PAN-FRIED MARYLAND CRAB CAKES

This recipe showcases the crabmeat from Byrd's, our long-time supplier on the eastern shore of Maryland.
The recipe calls for only light binding and just the right blend of herbs and spices,
so be sure to use the best quality lump crab available.

3/4 cup finely *diced* onion
(1 small onion)

1/2 cup finely diced celery
(2 small ribs celery)

2 tablespoons unsalted butter

1 1/2 teaspoons dry mustard

1/8 teaspoon cayenne

1 pound cooked lump crabmeat,
picked over to remove any shell

1 egg

2/3 cup fresh bread crumbs

1/4 cup mayonnaise

2 tablespoons chopped fresh mint

2 tablespoons chopped
fresh cilantro

1 1/2 teaspoons Old Bay
seafood seasoning

1 teaspoon grated lemon *zest*

Salt, to taste

Clarified butter or oil
(such as canola, soy or safflower),
for frying

1. In a medium sauté pan, *sauté* the onion and celery in the butter over medium heat until soft but not brown, 4-5 minutes. Add the mustard and cayenne and stir well; let the mixture cool.

2. In a bowl, combine all the remaining ingredients (except the clarified butter) with the cooled vegetable mixture; do not overmix.

3. Heat some clarified butter in a heavy-bottomed sauté pan. Scoop out about 1/3 cup of the mixture and shape into a loose patty. Repeat until all the patties are made. Fry over medium heat, pressing down lightly with a spatula. Cook until the crab cakes are golden brown and crispy, about 3 minutes on each side. Serve hot with a lemon wedge or some Spicy Remoulade Sauce, p. 88.

Makes 8 3-inch cakes

PAN-SEARED SCALLOPS
ON RED ONION MARMALADE

A study in contrasts, this dish pairs the sweet ivory flesh of sea scallops
with a tangy garnet-colored onion marmalade — we often present it as an hors d'oeuvre, too.

2 1/2 pounds sea scallops

For the marinade:

1 cup water

1/4 cup lemon juice

2 tablespoons brown sugar

1 tablespoon Worcestershire sauce

1 1/2 teaspoons ground ginger

1/2 teaspoon salt

1/4 teaspoon white pepper

For the marmalade:

3 tablespoons extra-virgin olive oil

4 pounds red onions, thinly sliced (10 cups)

1 tablespoon brown sugar

Salt and white pepper, to taste

3/4 cup red wine vinegar

1 1/4 cups red wine

Oil (such as canola, soy or safflower), for frying

2 tablespoons chopped fresh chives

1. Rinse the scallops. With your fingers, peel away the small tab of tough connective tissue on the side of each scallop. In a bowl large enough to accommodate all the scallops, mix together the marinade ingredients. Add the scallops and toss to coat thoroughly. Marinate in the refrigerator about 30 minutes.

2. Make the red onion marmalade: heat the olive oil in a large heavy-bottomed saucepan and add the onions. Cook over medium heat until they begin to soften, about 10 minutes, then add the brown sugar and stir to coat. Season with salt and pepper. Continue cooking over medium heat, stirring frequently, until the onions are golden brown, another 10-15 minutes. Add the vinegar and cook until it has completely evaporated, then add the red wine and repeat the process, stirring the onions frequently to prevent sticking and burning. When the red wine has evaporated, taste and correct the seasoning. Remove from the heat and keep warm. (The marmalade may be made up to 2 days ahead.)

3. Drain the scallops and pat dry with paper towels. Heat a non-stick frying pan until very hot. With a paper towel, rub a thin film of oil on the pan, then add the scallops in a single layer. **Sear** over high heat until just barely opaque in the center, 3-4 minutes on each side for large scallops. (Cook in batches if necessary to avoid crowding the pan and ensure proper searing.) To serve, arrange the warm onion marmalade on a warmed platter or plates. Arrange the hot scallops on top, sprinkle with the chopped chives and serve immediately.

Serves 8

Poultry

DRAPER'S CAFE CHICKEN POT PIE

This homey dish—perfect for lunch or a light supper—was a favorite of Dorothy Draper's, and is featured at her namesake cafe. Unlike a traditional "pot pie", in this recipe the pastry crust is baked separately so it stays flaky and crisp.

1 3-pound chicken

4 tablespoons (1/2 stick) unsalted butter

1 cup *diced* carrots (2 medium carrots)

1 cup sliced celery (3 medium ribs celery)

1 cup diced onion (1 medium onion)

1 cup quartered common mushrooms (2 ounces)

Salt and freshly ground black pepper, to taste

6 tablespoons all-purpose flour

1/2 cup dry white wine

3 cups *chicken stock,* preferably homemade

1 cup half-and-half or light cream

1 pound homemade or prepared frozen *puff pastry,* thawed

1. Put the chicken in a stock pot with lightly salted cold water to cover. Bring to a boil, reduce the heat and **poach** gently, skimming frequently, until the chicken is very tender when pierced with a knife, 45-55 minutes. Leave to cool in the poaching liquid. When cool enough to handle, remove all the meat, using a paring knife and your fingers. Discard any skin, fat or gristle. Cut the meat into 1-inch dice. (Note: the poaching liquid can be used as the chicken stock. **Reduce** the stock by boiling it down if necessary to ensure a full flavor.)

2. In a large heavy-bottomed saucepan, heat half the butter and *sauté* the carrots, celery and onion over medium heat until they are beginning to soften, 5-7 minutes. Add the mushrooms and continue cooking until their liquid has been rendered and evaporated, another 3-4 minutes. Season to taste with salt and pepper.

3. Add the remaining butter, stir until melted, then sprinkle the flour over the vegetables. Cook, stirring constantly for about 2 minutes, then add the white wine. Stir to dissolve any lumps of flour, then add the chicken stock and stir until combined. Reduce the heat and simmer until the vegetables are very tender and the sauce has thickened, about 15 more minutes. Add the half-and-half and bring to a boil. Add the chopped chicken, cook for a few more minutes to heat through. Season to taste with salt and pepper.

4. Preheat the oven to 400F. Roll out the puff pastry to 1/8-inch and cut out 8 circles the same diameter as the serving bowls. Place the pastry circles on an ungreased baking sheet and prick the entire surface with the tines of a fork. (The pastry circles should be flaky but not risen too high). Bake in the preheated oven until deep golden brown and slightly puffed, about 20 minutes.

5. To serve, divide the hot chicken mixture between 8 individual serving bowls and top with a puff pastry circle.

Serves 8

GREENBRIER CHICKEN SALAD

A perennial favorite at The Greenbrier that tastes especially good on the sandwiches at the Golf Course Halfway Houses! We use very flavorful fowl, but ordinary chicken will work well.

1 5-pound fowl or 2 2¹/₂-pound
chickens

1 cup *diced* celery
(3 medium ribs celery)

²/₃ cup sour cream

1¹/₃ cups mayonnaise

2 tablespoons white wine vinegar

Salt and freshly ground black
pepper, to taste

1. Put the chickens in a large stock pot with lightly salted cold water to cover. Bring to a boil, reduce the heat and *poach* gently, skimming off any foam accumulating on the surface, until the meat is very tender when pierced with a knife, 50-60 minutes. Leave the chickens to cool in the poaching liquid. When cool enough to handle, remove all the meat, using a paring knife and your fingers. Discard any skin, fat or gristle. Cut the meat into ¹/₂-inch dice. (The poaching liquid can be used as chicken stock in another recipe.) The chicken may be prepared up to 1 day ahead.

2. Mix together the diced chicken, diced celery, sour cream, mayonnaise and vinegar. Season to taste with salt and pepper. Chill well before serving, with greens and vegetables as a salad, on bread for a sandwich or with half a cantaloupe, as served at The Greenbrier outdoor pool.

Serves 8

SOUTHERN FRIED CHICKEN

Everyone has a secret recipe for fried chicken, and we're happy to share ours because we think it's the best. Our two-step cooking method produces a chicken with a minimum of fat, and frying in clarified butter ensures a deep golden crust.

1 3½-pound chicken, cut into 8 pieces (2 breast halves, 2 wings, 2 thighs, 2 drumsticks)

2 medium cloves garlic, put through a press or minced to a fine puree

Salt and freshly ground black pepper, to taste

½ cup heavy cream

Flour, for dredging

Clarified butter, for frying

1. Preheat the oven to 375F. Rub the chicken pieces with the garlic and season with salt and pepper. Cover loosely with plastic wrap and refrigerate 15 minutes to absorb the flavors.

2. Put the cream in a shallow bowl and the flour on a plate. Dip each chicken piece in the cream, shake off the excess, then dredge in the flour to coat, patting to remove the excess. Let the pieces dry on a rack or baking sheet for 10-15 minutes for a crispier coating.

3. Heat the clarified butter in a large skillet (filled to a depth of ½ inch) until hot. Fry the chicken pieces until golden brown, turning to brown all sides, 10 - 12 minutes. Transfer the chicken to a rack placed over a roasting pan or baking sheet and continue cooking in the preheated oven until the chicken is tender and the juice runs clear when pierced with a knife, 25-30 more minutes. Serve hot or at room temperature.

Makes 8 pieces

ROAST CHICKEN BREAST GREENBRIER VALLEY

The Greenbrier Valley offers an abundance of fresh produce, including the chanterelles and other wild mushrooms that give this dish its outstanding flavor.

1 tablespoon chopped shallot
(1/2 medium shallot)

1 tablespoon unsalted butter

1 cup chopped chanterelles
or other mushrooms, preferably
wild (3 ounces)

1 small clove garlic, minced

1 tablespoon madeira or port

Salt and freshly ground black
pepper, to taste

1 cup loosely packed de-stemmed
fresh spinach leaves, or
1 tablespoon frozen
spinach, thawed

8 ounces raw boneless skinless
chicken meat (light or dark),
cut in chunks

1 egg white, chilled

1/2 cup heavy cream, chilled

1 tablespoon chopped mixed fresh
herbs (such as parsley, chives,
tarragon, chervil)

2 tablespoons cooked and drained
corn kernels

8 single chicken breasts, skin on,
preferably still on the bone

Melted butter for brushing

1. In a small sauté pan, cook the shallot in half the butter over medium heat until soft but not brown, about 2 minutes. Add the *wild mushrooms* and *sauté* over medium heat until all the moisture has evaporated, 4-5 minutes. Add the garlic and madeira and cook until dry. Season to taste with salt and pepper, then cool.

2. Melt the remaining butter in a small saucepan, add the spinach and toss with a fork until the leaves are wilted and the liquid has been rendered. Remove the spinach from the pan and squeeze out any remaining liquid. Chop finely and cool.

3. Puree the boneless chicken meat in a food processor; add the egg white and process a few seconds more. Transfer the mixture to a metal or glass bowl set in a large bowl of ice (the mixture must stay very cold). Use a wooden spoon and beat in the cream a little at a time, making sure the cream is fully incorporated before adding more. Season with a generous pinch of salt and pepper.

4. Preheat the oven to 425F. Stir the cooled mushroom mixture, cooled spinach mixture, herbs and corn into the chicken mousse. (Keep this mixture cold until ready to use.) Slide your finger between the chicken skin and flesh to create a pocket. Spread some filling mixture under the skin of each breast (about 2 tablespoons) using a teaspoon or a piping bag with a plain large tip. Press down the skin to seal. Brush the breasts with melted butter, season with salt and pepper.

5. Place the chicken breasts on a baking sheet, skin side up, and roast in the preheated oven until golden brown and the juice runs clear when the breast is pricked, about 20 minutes. Remove from the oven, cover loosely with aluminum foil and leave in a warm place for 4-5 minutes to allow the juices to redistribute. Carefully cut or pull each breast half from the bone (if still attached), then slice into 3 diagonal portions and arrange on warmed plates.

Serves 8

CHICKEN BREASTS WITH VIRGINIA HAM AND HERBED CHEVRE

Chicken Cordon Bleu, Appalachian-style! Our creamy West Virginia-produced chevre and sweet cured ham transform this continental classic into a regional delight.

8 ounces fresh *chevre* cheese, softened at room temperature

2 tablespoons chopped mixed fresh herbs (such as parsley, dill, tarragon, chervil, chives)

Salt and freshly ground black pepper, to taste

8 large boneless skinless single chicken breasts (about 4 ounces each), or 16 small single breasts (about 2 ounces each)

8 thin slices *Virginia ham,* 4 inches by 2 inches each

Flour, seasoned to taste with salt and pepper, for dredging

2 eggs, lightly beaten

1 cup fresh bread crumbs

Clarified butter or oil (such as canola, soy or safflower), for frying

1 lemon, cut into 8 wedges

1. With a fork, mix the cheese, herbs, salt and pepper in a small bowl until well-combined.

2. Trim away any fat or membrane from the chicken breasts. For the large breasts, carefully cut along 1 long side of each breast with a sharp knife, forming a pocket by cutting deeply into the breast but not through the other side. For the small breasts, flatten them slightly with a back of a large knife. Spread the pocket (or 1 small breast half) with about 2 tablespoons of the cheese mixture. Lay a slice of the ham on the cheese. Close the pocket (or top with a second small breast) and press lightly to seal.

3. Put the seasoned flour in a shallow dish and the beaten egg in another one. Dredge the breasts in the flour, patting to remove any excess, then dip in the beaten eggs and roll in bread crumbs to coat completely. Lay the breasts on a tray and chill for 15 minutes. (This will help the crumb coating stay intact during cooking.)

4. Heat a large heavy-bottomed frying pan with 1/4 inch butter. Gently fry the chicken breasts until golden brown, 3-4 minutes on each side. Drain for a few seconds on paper towels, then arrange on warmed serving plates or a platter. Decorate with the lemon wedges.

Serves 8

HERB-SCENTED ROAST CHICKEN

In our Tavern Room we spit-roast whole free-range chickens on a French rotisserie.
Roasting in a conventional oven with the following method will yield tender flavorful results, too.

1 6-pound roasting chicken
or capon, or 2 3-pound
roasting chickens

1/2 small onion

Pared *zest* of 1 lemon

1 large sprig fresh rosemary or
1 teaspoon dried

1/4 cup extra-virgin olive oil

1 tablespoon chopped mixed
fresh herbs (such as thyme,
rosemary, basil, oregano), or
1 teaspoon dried

Salt and freshly ground black
pepper, to taste

1. Rinse the chicken and dry thoroughly with paper towels. Put the onion, lemon zest and rosemary in the cavity. Truss the chicken with kitchen twine or skewers, if you wish, so it holds its shape during cooking. Mix the olive oil and herbs and brush onto the chicken, then season generously with salt and pepper. Cover with plastic wrap and marinate in the refrigerator about 1 hour.

2. Preheat the oven to 400F. Place the marinated chicken on a rack in a roasting pan and roast in the preheated oven until tender when pierced with a knife and the juices from the body cavity run clear when the chicken is tilted, 1 - 1 1/4 hours. Remove from the oven, cover loosely with aluminum foil and leave to rest about 10 minutes before serving. Cut the trussing strings, remove the flavoring ingredients from the cavity and discard. Serve on a warmed platter, whole or carved into portions.

Serves 8

TURKEY SCALLOPINI WITH BLACK BEAN RELISH

This lively dish is low in fat and very colorful — the turkey cooks beautifully on an outdoor grill.

2¹/₂ pounds boneless turkey breast, cut in 16 thin scallopini (about 2¹/₂ ounces each) and pounded to a thickness of ¹/₄ inch

¹/₂ cup avocado oil or extra-virgin olive oil

3 medium cloves garlic, minced

2 tablespoons plus 1 teaspoon finely chopped or grated fresh ginger

Salt and freshly ground black pepper, to taste

¹/₄ cup rice vinegar or white wine vinegar

1¹/₂ cups cooked and drained black beans (1 15-ounce can)

1 cup *diced* red bell pepper (1 medium pepper)

1 cup cooked and drained corn (1 8-ounce can)

¹/₂ cup diced jicama

3 tablespoons chopped fresh cilantro or parsley

1 teaspoon finely chopped seeded jalapeno pepper

1. Arrange the turkey on a platter or tray, brush with ¹/₂ of the oil, sprinkle with ¹/₃ of the garlic and 2 tablespoons of the ginger. Season with salt and pepper, cover with plastic wrap and marinate in the refrigerator 1 hour.

2. In a medium bowl, whisk together the remaining oil with the vinegar. Add all the remaining ingredients and toss to mix thoroughly. Season to taste with salt and pepper. Cover. (The relish may be made up to 1 day ahead, refrigerated and brought back to room temperature before serving.)

3. Scrape off any excess marinade from the turkey. Heat a non-stick skillet or stove-top grill and quickly cook the turkey scallopini until just barely pink inside, about 1 minute on each side (the turkey will continue to cook slightly after removal from the pan). Arrange on warmed serving plates or a platter, spoon a little relish on top and serve immediately.

Serves 8

ROAST QUAIL STUFFED WITH SAVOY CABBAGE, WILD RICE AND MUSHROOMS

Most quail are sold partially-boned, making them easy to stuff and very easy to eat.

1/2 cup chopped shallot (4 medium shallots)	Salt and freshly ground black pepper, to taste
4 tablespoons unsalted butter	2 1/2 cups cooked wild rice
2 cloves garlic, minced	1 1/2 teaspoons chopped fresh thyme or 1/2 teaspoon dried
3 cups finely shredded Savoy cabbage	16 quail, partially-boned
1 1/2 cups chopped *wild mushrooms* (such as shiitake, chanterelle or morel, or a mix of common and wild) (4 ounces)	2 tablespoons oil (such as olive, canola or soy)

1. In a large saucepan, *sauté* the shallot in the butter until soft but not brown, about 2 minutes. Add the garlic and cook another minute, then add the cabbage and mushrooms and season with salt and pepper. Reduce the heat to very low, cover the pan and cook, stirring frequently, until the cabbage and mushrooms are very soft, 15-18 minutes. Add the cooked rice and the thyme. Taste and adjust seasoning, then leave to cool completely before stuffing the quail.

2. Preheat the oven to 400F. Season the inside and outside of the quail with salt and pepper, then fill the cavity with about 1/4 cup of the stuffing. Heat the oil in a sauté pan and brown the quail on all sides. Transfer to a roasting pan and roast the quail in the preheated oven until the juice runs clear when the quail is pricked with a skewer, about 12 minutes. Transfer to a warmed serving platter and serve immediately.

Serves 8

ROAST DUCK WITH GREENBRIER PEACHES

Roast duck with a fruit garnish is a classic combination, particularly delicious with our succulent Greenbrier peaches! Take care to deglaze the roasting pan well for an intensely flavored sauce.

2 6-pound young ducks

Salt and freshly ground black pepper, to taste

1 tablespoon oil (such as canola, soy or safflower)

1 cup chopped onion (1 medium onion)

1 cup chopped carrot (2 medium carrots)

2/3 cup chopped celery (2 medium ribs celery)

3/4 cup chopped *leek* (1 medium leek, white part only)

1/2 cup cognac

6 cups full-bodied *duck, chicken or veal stock,* preferably homemade

1 *bouquet garni*

10 black peppercorns

1/4 cup peach juice, reserved from *Greenbrier peaches* (if using fresh peaches, 1/4 cup pureed and strained peaches)

1 1/2 teaspoons *arrowroot* dissolved in 2 tablespoons sherry vinegar or red wine vinegar

8 Greenbrier peach halves, or other large canned or fresh peaches

1. Preheat the oven to 400F. Remove the giblets from the inside of the ducks. Cut off the wing tips to the first joint and cut off the necks, if still attached. Trim any excess fat from the ducks, pat them dry inside and out and season well with salt and pepper. Truss the ducks with kitchen twine or skewers, if you wish, to keep their shape during cooking. Place the ducks on a rack in a roasting pan and roast in the preheated oven, rotating the ducks about every 30 minutes so they spend equal time on all sides. Roast until the skin is golden and crisp and the juices run clear from the body cavity when the ducks are tilted, about 2 hours for well-done.

2. While the ducks are roasting, chop the wing tips, neck and giblets (do not use the liver) into chunks. (If the ducks did not come with a neck or giblets, substitute some dark chicken or turkey meat—legs, thighs or necks.) Heat the oil in a large heavy-bottomed saucepan until very hot, and thoroughly brown the duck pieces and the chopped vegetables, stirring constantly to prevent sticking and burning. When the ingredients are well-browned, remove the pan from the heat, add the cognac and stir until the alcohol vapors have dissipated. Return the pan to the heat and cook until all the liquid has evaporated, scraping the bottom of the pan to dissolve all the caramelized juices. Add the stock, bouquet garni and peppercorns. Bring to a boil, reduce to a *simmer* and continue cooking, skimming away any foam or fat that accumulates on the surface, until the liquid is *reduced* in volume by 2/3. Taste and correct seasoning. (The sauce should be fairly intensely flavored and full-bodied at this point. If weak, continue to reduce until the desired intensity is achieved.)

3. Strain the sauce into a clean pan and add the peach juice. (If time permits, before adding the juice, chill the stock to allow any remaining fat to congeal on the surface for easy removal.)

4. When the ducks are cooked, remove them from the roasting pan, cover loosely with aluminum foil and let rest in a warm place for 10-12 minutes to allow the juices to redistribute before carving. Carefully pour off the fat from the roasting pan, keeping the caramelized juices and browned bits in the bottom. **_Deglaze_** the pan by adding a little stock or water and stirring over heat to dissolve. Strain these deglazed juices into the sauce. Taste and correct seasoning. Bring the sauce to a boil and whisk in the dissolved arrowroot to slightly thicken the sauce.

5. To serve, heat the peach halves in a little sauce. Place the roasted ducks on a warm serving platter. Arrange the warm peach halves around the ducks and serve. Pass the sauce separately.

Serves 8

Meat

NEW YORK STRIP WITH SHALLOT, LEMON, PEPPER CRUST AND WHOLE-GRAINED MUSTARD SAUCE

Be vigilant when sautéing the steaks so as not to burn the shallot coating.

8 8-ounce New York strip steaks, about ¾-inch thick

Salt

4 medium shallots, very thinly sliced (½ cup)

2 tablespoons coarsely crushed black peppercorns

Grated *zest* of 2 lemons (2 tablespoons)

6 tablespoons unsalted butter

½ cup cognac or brandy

1 cup *veal or chicken stock,* preferably homemade

¾ cup heavy cream

3 tablespoons whole-grained mustard

Juice from 1 lemon

Freshly ground black pepper, to taste

1. Season the steaks with salt on both sides. Combine the shallots, crushed peppercorns and lemon zest in a small bowl. Press about 1½ tablespoons of the mixture onto 1 side of each steak.

2. In a heavy sauté pan large enough to fit 4 steaks, heat half the butter and *sauté* the steaks over medium heat, coated side first, until browned, about 4 minutes. Carefully turn over the steaks and sauté on the other side, about 4 more minutes for medium rare. (The steaks will continue to cook a little bit after they are removed from the pan.) Repeat with the remaining butter and steaks. Transfer the finished steaks to a platter, cover loosely with aluminum foil and keep warm while making the sauce.

3. Remove the pan from the heat, pour off any excess fat from the pan and add the brandy. Stir off the heat until the alcohol vapors have dissipated, then return to high heat and boil until *reduced* to a syrupy glaze, scraping with a wooden spoon to dissolve all the caramelized juices from the steaks. Add the stock and continue to boil until reduced by half, then add the cream and boil until the sauce has reduced to a coating consistency, another 3-4 minutes. Add the mustard and lemon juice and season to taste with salt and pepper. Arrange the steaks on warmed plates or a platter and pass the sauce separately.

Serves 8

TAVERN BEEF STROGANOFF

A classic beef preparation enjoyed by Tavern diners for many years.

2¹/2 pounds beef tenderloin, cut into 2-inch x ¹/2-inch strips

1 teaspoon mild paprika

Salt and freshly ground black pepper, to taste

6 tablespoons unsalted butter

2 cups thinly sliced common mushrooms (5 ounces)

¹/2 cup chopped shallot (3 medium shallots)

3 tablespoons all-purpose flour

³/4 cup dry white wine

1 cup *veal or beef stock,* preferably homemade

³/4 cup sour cream

¹/2 cup *julienne* of dill pickle

1. Sprinkle the beef with the paprika, salt and pepper, tossing to coat evenly. In a large sauté pan, heat half of the butter and *sauté* the beef over high heat until just browned on the outside but rare on the inside, about 1 minute (do this in batches if necessary to avoid crowding the pan). Set the meat aside.

2. Add the remaining butter to the sauté pan and sauté the mushrooms until all their liquid has been rendered and evaporated, 4-5 minutes. Add the shallots and continue to sauté until they are soft and the mushrooms are slightly brown, another 2-3 minutes.

3. Sprinkle the flour over the mushrooms and stir until mixed. Add the wine, stirring to avoid lumps, and boil for about 1 minute, then add the stock, reduce the heat and *simmer* until slightly thickened, about 10 minutes. Remove from the heat, stir in the sour cream, add the meat and any accumulated juices. Return to low heat and cook for a few more minutes to warm the meat. (Once the sour cream is added, do not boil or it will curdle.) Taste and correct seasoning. Transfer the stroganoff to a warmed serving bowl and garnish with the pickle julienne. Serve with egg noodles.

Serves 8

VEAL NOISETTES WITH CHANTERELLES AND DILL VINAIGRETTE

Tender veal, nutty chanterelles and tangy dill harmonize deliciously in this unusual dish.
If chanterelles are not available, common mushrooms would be good too —
be sure to sauté them until golden brown and crisp.

2¹/2 pounds veal tenderloin, cut into ³/4-inch slices

Salt and freshly ground black pepper, to taste

2 teaspoons oil (such as olive, canola or soy)

2 tablespoons unsalted butter

1 pound chanterelles, thinly sliced (8 cups)

2 medium shallots (2 ounces), minced

¹/2 cup white wine vinegar

¹/2 cup extra-virgin olive oil

1 tablespoon chopped fresh dill or 1 teaspoon dried dill

1. Season the veal with salt and pepper. In a large sauté pan (preferably not a non-stick pan), heat the oil and *sauté* the veal over medium-high heat until just pink inside, 2-3 minutes on each side. Remove the pan from the heat, transfer the veal to a plate, cover and keep warm.

2. Return the same sauté pan to medium heat and sauté the chanterelles in the butter until they have rendered all their liquid and are crispy and golden brown, 6-8 minutes. Season to taste with salt and pepper. Add the shallots and continue to sauté 1-2 more minutes. Remove them from the pan and keep warm.

3. Add the white wine vinegar to the pan and boil until *reduced* to 3 spoonfuls of syrupy glaze, stirring to dissolve all the caramelized juices in the bottom of the pan. Whisk in the olive oil while the sauce is boiling, then add the chopped dill. Season to taste with salt and pepper.

4. Pour any accumulated veal juices into the vinaigrette and whisk to re-emulsify if necessary. Arrange the veal noisettes on warmed serving plates. Spoon the chanterelles on top and drizzle them with vinaigrette.

Serves 8

VEAL FRICASSEE A LA RUSCH

This dish tastes as delicious made today as it did 25 years ago when the Greenbrier's cuisine was very classically oriented under the leadership of Food Director Hermann Rusch.

2½ pounds boneless veal shoulder, trimmed of all fat and sinew, cut into 1-inch cubes

3 cups *chicken or light veal stock,* preferably homemade

2 cups dry white wine

1 cup chopped onion (1 medium onion)

1 *bouquet garni*

5 tablespoons unsalted butter

¼ cup all-purpose flour

1 cup heavy cream

Salt and white pepper, to taste

4 cups quartered common mushrooms (8 ounces)

¼ cup drained capers

2 tablespoons chopped fresh parsley

1. Put the veal in a large saucepan or stock pot and add the stock, wine, onion and bouquet garni. Bring to a *simmer* and cook, skimming frequently to remove any foam, until the veal is very tender, about 40 minutes. With a slotted spoon, remove the pieces of veal from the broth and set aside.

2. In another large saucepan, cook 4 tablespoons of the butter and the flour together for 2-3 minutes, whisking constantly, to form a smooth *roux.* Strain the broth into the roux, whisking rapidly to avoid lumps. Bring to a boil, add the cream and reduce the heat. Simmer until the sauce is slightly *reduced* and thickened, about 10 more minutes.

3. In a medium sauté pan, *sauté* the mushrooms over medium high heat in the remaining tablespoon of butter until their liquid has been rendered and evaporated and they are golden brown, about 8 minutes. Season to taste with salt and pepper. Add the sautéed mushrooms and the reserved veal to the sauce and simmer to heat through. Taste and correct seasoning. To serve, ladle the stew into a warmed serving bowl and sprinkle with the capers and chopped parsley. Serve hot with Mushroom Spatzle (p. 148), rice or buttered noodles.

Serves 8

THE TAVERN BROILED VEAL CHOPS
WITH MOREL SAUCE

A magnificent pairing of tender juicy veal and earthy morels makes this dish a meat-lover's delight.
It has been a specialty of the Tavern menu since the opening of the restaurant in 1970.

**2 tablespoons minced shallot
(1 small shallot)**

2 teaspoons unsalted butter

**1½ cups chopped morels, cleaned
of all sand and grit (if using
dried morels, soften by soaking
in hot water for 20 minutes,
then measure)**

½ cup dry white wine

2 cups heavy cream

**2 teaspoons *glace de viande,* or
¾ cup *reduced veal or beef stock,*
preferably homemade**

**Salt and freshly ground black
pepper, to taste**

**8 8-ounce veal loin chops,
1 inch thick**

1. In a medium sauté pan, ***sauté*** the shallot in the butter over medium heat until soft but not brown, about 3 minutes. Add the morels and sauté lightly, 2-3 minutes. Add the wine and cook over high heat until only 2 spoonfuls of liquid remain. Add the cream and the glace de viande or reduced stock. Continue to boil until the sauce has a rich, coating consistency and is reduced in volume to 2 cups. Season to taste with salt and pepper. Keep warm. (The sauce may be made up to 1 day ahead.)

2. Preheat the broiler. Season the chops with salt and pepper to taste. Put the chops on a broiling pan and broil 2 inches from the heat until just a trace of pink remains in the center, 4-5 minutes on each side for medium. Remove the chops from the broiler, cover loosely with aluminum foil and let rest in a warm place for 3-4 minutes more to let the juices redistribute for better texture. Pour any accumulated juices into the sauce. Arrange the chops on a warmed platter or plates, pour a little sauce over them and pass the rest.

Serves 8

LOIN OF LAMB WITH HONEY, LEMON AND THYME

*This dish is featured as one of our special Gold Service Dinner selections
and is pictured on the cover of this book.*

2¹/₂ pounds boneless loin of lamb

Salt and freshly ground black
pepper, to taste

Grated *zest* of 1 lemon

1 tablespoon chopped fresh thyme
or 1 teaspoon dried

2 tablespoons oil
(such as olive, canola or soy)

4 tablespoons honey

1 cup *lamb or veal stock,*
preferably homemade

¹/₄ cup red wine

12 tablespoons (1¹/₂ sticks)
unsalted butter, cut in pieces

1. Preheat the oven to 400F. Season the lamb loins with salt and pepper, then rub with the lemon zest and thyme. Heat the oil in a sauté pan and brown the lamb pieces well on all sides. Pour off any excess fat, then pour the honey over the browned lamb in the pan, turning it to coat thoroughly. Remove the pan from the heat; place the lamb in a roasting pan and transfer to the preheated oven. Roast until medium rare, about 8-10 minutes. (The internal temperature should be 125F.)

2. Return the sauté pan to the heat and add the stock and red wine. Bring to a boil and boil until *reduced* by about half, scraping with a wooden spoon to dissolve any caramelized meat juices and honey. Whisk in the butter, bit by bit, to form a creamy sauce. Taste and correct seasoning, then strain through a fine-meshed strainer and keep warm.

3. Remove the lamb from the oven, cover with aluminum foil and let rest 4 - 5 minutes. Pour any accumulated juices into the sauce, then slice the lamb and arrange on warmed plates or a platter. Pour a little warm sauce over the meat and pass the rest separately.

Serves 8

GREENBRIER LAMB STEW

This rosemary-scented stew has an unthickened broth — almost like a soup.

2¹/2 pounds boneless lamb shoulder, trimmed of fat and sinew and cut into 1-inch cubes

6 cups *chicken or lamb stock,* preferably homemade

1 *bouquet garni,* including 2 large sprigs fresh rosemary or 1¹/2 teaspoons dried

1¹/2 pounds potatoes, peeled and cut into 1-inch chunks

1 medium onion (6 ounces), cut in large *dice*

2 medium ribs celery (3 ounces), cut into 1-inch pieces

4 medium carrots (8 ounces), cut into 1-inch pieces

2 cloves garlic, chopped

Salt and freshly ground black pepper, to taste

2 tablespoons chopped fresh parsley

1. **Blanch** the lamb by placing it in a large saucepan, covering with cold water, bringing to a boil and draining it. Transfer the blanched meat to a stockpot. Add the stock and bouquet garni. Bring to a *simmer* and cook until the meat is fairly tender, about 45 minutes, skimming off any foam or fat that accumulates on the surface. (Do not let the stock come to a full boil or the meat will toughen.)

2. When the lamb is fairly tender, add the potatoes, onion, celery, carrots and garlic. Season to taste with salt and pepper and continue to simmer until the vegetables and meat are both very tender, about 30 minutes more. Remove and discard the bouquet garni. Taste and correct seasoning. To serve, transfer the stew to a warmed tureen or serving bowls and sprinkle on a little chopped parsley (the stew will be very "brothy".)

Serves 8

RACK OF LAMB GREENBRIER

*Tender young lamb from neighboring Monroe County
gets regal treatment in this classic roast lamb preparation.*

1 cup fresh bread crumbs	3 trimmed lamb racks (6 chops each, about 2 per person)
1 cup loosely-packed fresh parsley sprigs	1 tablespoon oil (such as olive, canola or soy)
1 medium clove garlic, crushed	1 egg
1 tablespoon chopped fresh rosemary or 1 teaspoon dried	2 tablespoons prepared mustard
Salt and freshly ground black pepper, to taste	2 tablespoons unsalted butter, melted

1. Combine the bread crumbs, parsley, garlic, rosemary, salt and pepper in a food processor and work until thoroughly mixed. (Alternatively, finely chop all ingredients by hand and stir to combine.)

2. Preheat the oven to 400F. Season the lamb racks with salt and pepper. Heat the oil in a large sauté pan until quite hot and *sear* the racks on all sides until thoroughly and evenly browned. (Do this in batches if necessary.) Remove the lamb from the pan and leave until cool enough to handle.

3. Mix the egg and mustard together until smooth. Spread over the fat sides of the cooled lamb. Coat the same sides with a thick layer of the crumb mixture, patting to help the crumbs adhere. Drizzle the melted butter over the crumb coating. Set the lamb on a roasting pan, coating side up, and roast in the preheated oven 20 minutes for medium rare. (The internal temperature should be 125F.)

4. Remove the lamb from the oven, cover loosely with aluminum foil and leave in a warm place for 5-7 minutes to let the juices redistribute for better texture. Cut the racks into individual chops and arrange on a warmed platter or plates, or present the racks of lamb whole on a warmed serving platter and carve at the table.

Serves 8

BROILED PORK CHOPS WITH
DRIED CHERRY COMPOTE

The cherry compote is also delicious with roast pork loin or grilled pork sausages.

3 pounds red onions, thinly
sliced (6 cups)

1 1/2 cups kiln-dried cherries

1/2 cup red wine

1/4 cup red wine vinegar

1/4 cup granulated sugar

2-inch strip pared orange *zest*

Salt and freshly ground black
pepper, to taste

1 tablespoon chopped fresh thyme
or 1 teaspoon dried

8 1-inch thick pork chops

2 tablespoons extra-virgin
olive oil

1. Combine the onions, cherries, wine, vinegar, sugar, orange zest, salt, pepper and 1/4 teaspoon of the thyme in a heavy-bottomed saucepan, bring to a boil, stirring to dissolve the sugar. Reduce the heat to a low *simmer,* cover the pan and cook until the onions and cherries are very soft and the liquid is thick and syrupy, about 30 minutes. Remove and discard the orange zest. Taste and correct seasoning. Keep warm. (The compote may be made up to 3 days ahead.)

2. Preheat the broiler. Brush the chops with the olive oil and season with the remaining thyme, salt and pepper. Leave for about 15 minutes to absorb the flavors. Put the chops on a broiling pan and broil 2 inches from the heat until just a trace of pink remains, about 5 minutes on each side. Transfer the chops to a platter, cover loosely with aluminum foil and keep warm. Let rest for 3 - 4 minutes to allow the chops to finish cooking and the juices to redistribute for better texture. Arrange on warmed plates with a spoonful of warm cherry compote.

Serves 8

TARBORO BARBECUE PORK

The Greenbrier developed this recipe after tasting a fabulous barbecue from this region of North Carolina. The marinade and sauce is tangy with vinegar and has only a hint of ketchup.

1¹/₃ cups cider vinegar

1¹/₂ cups water

²/₃ cup ketchup

6 tablespoons brown sugar

1 tablespoon salt

1 tablespoon granulated sugar

2 teaspoons freshly ground black pepper

1¹/₂ teaspoons crushed red pepper flakes

1 4-pound boneless pork shoulder (picnic)

1. In a bowl large enough to fit the pork, stir all the ingredients (except the pork) together until the sugar is dissolved. Remove and reserve 1 cup of the mixture to use as a sauce for the finished meat. With a sharp knife, make several deep slits in the pork, to help the marinade penetrate. Place the pork in the marinade, cover and marinate 24 hours, turning frequently for even coverage.

2. Preheat the oven to 475F. Remove the pork from the marinade and place on a rack in a roasting pan. Roast in the preheated oven for 10 minutes, then reduce the heat to 250F. Continue to cook the pork until it is extremely tender, basting frequently with the marinade in which the pork has soaked, about 5 hours.

3. When the pork is cooked, remove it from the oven and leave until cool enough to handle. Cut it into thick slices, then shred it with your fingers or a fork. Mix the warm shredded meat with some of the reserved marinade to moisten it and serve piled on a platter for sandwiches. The pork may also be cut into thin slices, *simmered* for a few minutes in the reserved marinade and served on a platter. The Marinated Slaw on page 141 is a nice accompaniment.

Serves 8

VENISON RAGOUT WITH PINOT NOIR AND LINGONBERRIES

This wine-laced stew is much like a classic boeuf bourguignonne, so beef chuck or top round is an equally delicious replacement for the venison.

For the marinade:

2 cups chopped onion
(2 medium onions)

1 cup chopped carrots
(2 medium carrots)

1 medium clove garlic, crushed

1 bay leaf

2 sprigs fresh thyme or
1 teaspoon dried

1 sprig fresh rosemary or
1/2 teaspoon dried

1 teaspoon juniper berries,
crushed

1 bottle (3 cups) pinot noir or
other dry but fruity red wine

2 pounds venison sirloin or
top round, trimmed of all fat and
sinew and cut into 1-inch cubes

Salt and freshly ground black
pepper, to taste

2 tablespoons oil (such as olive,
canola or soy)

1/2 cup all-purpose flour

1 *bouquet garni*

6 cups full-bodied *venison or veal
stock,* preferably homemade

10 ounces carrots (5 medium
carrots), cut into 2-inch by
1/2-inch sticks

8 ounces pearl onions, trimmed
and cut in half if large

12 ounces celery root, cut into
1/2-inch *dice*

1 tablespoon unsalted butter

8 ounces common mushrooms,
quartered (4 cups)

1/2 cup lingonberry preserves

1. Combine the marinade ingredients and the venison in a large bowl, cover and marinate in the refrigerator for 24 hours.

2. Drain off the marinade liquid and reserve. Separate the meat from the vegetables, discarding the vegetables. Blot the meat dry with paper towels and season generously with salt and pepper. Heat the oil until quite hot in a large heavy-bottomed pan and brown the venison. (Be sure not to crowd the pan as this will prevent effective browning. Add the meat in batches, with another tablespoon of oil, if necessary.)

3. When all the meat is thoroughly browned, return it to the pan and sprinkle it with the flour, stirring to mix the flour with the accumulated fat, making a *roux*. Cook 1-2 minutes until the roux is light brown. Add the reserved marinade liquid, bouquet garni and stock. Season to taste with salt and pepper. Reduce the heat, cover and *simmer* gently until the meat is slightly tender when pierced with a knife, about 1 1/4 hours.

continued

4. Add the carrot sticks, pearl onions and diced celery root to the ragout and continue cooking until all the vegetables and meat are very tender, another 20-30 minutes.

5. Heat the butter in a sauté pan and *sauté* the quartered mushrooms until they have rendered their liquid and are golden brown. Season to taste with salt and pepper. Add to the ragout. Add the lingonberry preserves and stir to mix thoroughly. Taste and correct seasoning. Serve hot with Parmesan Polenta (page 149) or Mushroom Spatzle (page 148).

Serves 8

SAUTEED CALF'S LIVER WITH CARAMEL AND THYME GLAZE

This recipe elevates an often-maligned meat to new heights of flavor.
Be ready with all your ingredients — you must work quickly at the stove when making the glaze.

2¹/2 pounds calf's liver, cut into 16 thin scallops, each about 2¹/2 ounces

Salt and freshly ground black pepper, to taste

Flour, for dredging

8 tablespoons (1 stick) unsalted butter

3 tablespoons granulated sugar

¹/4 cup cider vinegar or sherry vinegar

³/4 cup brandy or cognac

2 teaspoons chopped fresh thyme or ¹/2 teaspoon dried

1. Season the liver with salt and pepper, then dredge in the flour to coat, patting to remove excess. Heat 2 tablespoons of the butter in a large heavy skillet and quickly *sauté* the liver over medium-high heat until it is *seared,* about 1 minute on each side. (Cook the liver in batches if necessary; crowding the pan will prevent proper searing.) Remove the pan from the heat, transfer the liver to a dish, cover with aluminum foil and keep warm.

2. Pour off any excess fat from the pan and return to medium-high heat. Add the sugar and stir with a wooden spoon until melted and a deep caramel color. Remove the pan from the heat and add the vinegar and brandy. Stir off the heat until the alcohol vapors have dissipated, then return to the heat. Stir to dissolve the caramel and boil until *reduced* to a few spoonfuls of syrupy glaze. Add the thyme and the remaining butter, swirling the pan to melt and incorporate the butter into the sauce.

3. Pour any accumulated juices into the sauce. Arrange the liver scallops on warmed plates or a platter, pour the sauce over and serve immediately.

Serves 8

Accompaniments

VEGETABLE RAGOUT WITH WILD MUSHROOM BUTTER

This complex blend of simmered vegetables makes a perfect complement to simply prepared meats or poultry. Use whatever seasonal vegetables you wish, keeping the color mix in mind and adding the quicker-cooking vegetables last.

1 small onion (4 ounces), sliced

2 tablespoons unsalted butter

4 medium carrots (8 ounces), cut into 2-inch by 1/4-inch sticks

1/2 medium cauliflower (1 pound), broken into florets

1 cup *chicken stock*, preferably homemade

Salt and freshly ground black pepper, to taste

3 medium yellow squash (1 pound), cut into 1-inch *dice*

8 ounces sugar snap peas, trimmed

1 medium red bell pepper (6 ounces), cut into *julienne*

1 small head raddichio (2 ounces), cut into *chiffonade*

4 - 6 tablespoons wild mushroom butter (see following recipe), or to taste

1 tablespoon chopped fresh parsley

1. In a large saucepan, cook the onion in the butter over medium heat until soft but not brown, about 3 minutes. Add the carrots, cauliflower and chicken stock. Season with salt and pepper. Reduce the heat, cover and simmer over low heat until the vegetables are slightly soft, about 10 minutes. Add the squash, sugar snaps and red peppers and continue to cook until all the vegetables are soft, another 8 - 10 minutes (add a little more stock if the vegetables are sticking). Add the raddichio chiffonade, stir and simmer until it is wilted, 2-3 minutes.

2. Remove the ragout from the heat. Add the wild mushroom butter, stir to mix, taste and correct seasoning. Transfer to a warmed serving bowl and sprinkle with the chopped parsley.

Serves 8

Wild Mushroom Butter

As this recipe makes more than needed for the ragout, store the excess in the freezer and slice off a round to top plain steamed vegetables or broiled fish.

4 ounces *wild mushrooms,* such as shiitake or chanterelle

16 tablespoons (2 sticks) unsalted butter, softened at room temperature

2 tablespoons chopped fresh parsley

1 tablespoon chopped mixed fresh herbs (such as tarragon, dill, chervil, basil, rosemary, chives)

1 small clove garlic, minced

1 1/2 teaspoons brandy

1 teaspoon Worcestershire sauce

Juice of 1/2 lemon

Salt and freshly ground black pepper, to taste

1. Chop the mushrooms in a food processor, using the pulse button, until very fine (alternatively, chop with a large knife). In a medium sauté pan, cook the mushrooms in 2 teaspoons of the butter over medium heat until they are soft and all their liquid has been rendered and evaporated, about 5 minutes. Transfer to a strainer and allow to drain and cool completely.

2. Combine the cooled mushrooms with the remaining ingredients and mix well in the food processor or with a wooden spoon. The butter may be shaped into a cylinder with plastic wrap, chilled or frozen, and sliced into rounds for serving. The butter may be kept up to 1 week in the refrigerator or 2 months in the freezer.

Makes 1/2 pound

RATATOUILLE-FILLED TOMATOES

If you don't want to stuff the tomatoes, just double the
filling quantities and serve as traditional ratatouille.

8 small tomatoes, cored and cut in
half lengthwise

1/2 small eggplant (6 ounces),
peeled, cut into 1/4-inch *dice*
and *degorged*

2 tablespoons extra-virgin
olive oil

1 large *tomato* (12 ounces), *peeled,*
seeded and cut into 1/2-inch dice

1/2 medium onion, chopped
(1/2 cup)

1 small zucchini (5 ounces), cut
into 1/4-inch dice

1 small yellow squash (5 ounces),
cut into 1/4-inch dice

1 garlic clove, minced

1/2 cup *chicken stock*

1 tablespoon tomato paste

1 tablespoon chopped mixed
fresh herbs (such as parsley,
basil, oregano)

Salt and freshly ground black
pepper, to taste

2 tablespoons freshly grated
Parmesan

1. With a teaspoon, scrape out the interior of the tomato halves to form 16 cups.
Place cut side down on a rack or plate and leave to drain until ready to fill.

2. Preheat the oven to 350F. Blot the eggplant dry with a paper towel. Heat the
oil in a large sauté pan, then *sauté* the eggplant over high heat about 3 minutes.
Add the diced tomato, onion, zucchini and yellow squash and continue to sauté,
shaking the pan to prevent sticking, until the vegetables start to brown slightly,
4-5 more minutes.

3. Add the garlic, chicken stock and tomato paste and *simmer* until the liquid is
reduced to a few tablespoons, 2-3 minutes. Remove from the heat, stir in the herbs
and season to taste with salt and pepper.

4. Season the inside of the tomato cups with salt and pepper. Spoon the ratatouille
into the cups and sprinkle the tops with a little Parmesan cheese. Arrange the
cups on a baking sheet or in a roasting pan and bake until the tomatoes are
warmed through and the cheese is golden brown, about 15 minutes. Serve hot or
at room temperature.

Serves 8

ROASTED EGGPLANT AND GARLIC TIMBALES

*Roasting the garlic greatly mellows its bite, but don't let it get too dark —
light gold and very soft to the touch will give the desired flavor.*

1¹/₂ pounds eggplant
(2 small eggplants)

Oil (such as canola, safflower or
soy), for brushing

6 medium cloves garlic, unpeeled

6 eggs

2 cups heavy cream

Pinch freshly ground nutmeg

Salt and freshly ground black
pepper, to taste

1. Preheat the oven to 375F. Grease 8 4-ounce timbale molds or ramekins. Pierce the eggplants several times with a sharp knife, brush them with oil, place them in a roasting pan and roast in the preheated oven for 20 minutes. Add the garlic cloves to the pan and continue roasting until the eggplant is very soft and slightly collapsed and the garlic is very soft, about 15 more minutes. Remove and leave until cool enough to handle. Reduce the oven temperature to 325F.

2. Cut the eggplant in half, scoop out enough pulp to measure 2 cups and put in a food processor. Squeeze the softened garlic from the skins into the food processor with all the remaining ingredients and process to form a very smooth puree. Fill the greased molds with the batter and set in a **water bath.** Bake until the timbales are fairly firm and a skewer inserted in the center comes out clean, 50-60 minutes. Remove from the water bath and cool about 10 minutes, then invert onto warmed serving plates or a platter and serve immediately.

Makes 8 4-ounce timbales

WARM ASPARAGUS WITH CHAMPAGNE CHANTERELLE VINAIGRETTE

If fresh chanterelles are not available, try another mild-flavored wild variety or use common mushrooms.

6 tablespoons minced shallot
(2 medium shallots)

½ cup extra-virgin olive oil

1½ cups finely *diced* chanterelles
(4 ounces)

½ cup *chicken stock,*
preferably homemade

¼ cup champagne vinegar

1 tablespoon whole-grained
mustard

2 tablespoons chopped fresh herbs
(such as dill, chervil, parsley,
tarragon, basil)

Salt and freshly ground black
pepper, to taste

2 pounds asparagus (green, white
or a mix), woody ends trimmed

1. In a small saucepan, cook the shallots with 1 tablespoon of the oil until soft but not brown, 3-4 minutes. Add the chanterelles and continue cooking until they have rendered their liquid and the liquid has evaporated, another 3-4 minutes. Add the stock and *simmer* until *reduced* by half, then add the vinegar.

2. Bring the vinaigrette to a boil and add the remaining olive oil bit by bit, whisking to emulsify. Remove from the heat, stir in the mustard and herbs and season to taste with salt and pepper. Keep warm.

3. With a vegetable peeler, strip off the outer layer of fibrous skin on each stalk of asparagus, from just below the tip to the end of the stalk. Gather the asparagus into 3 or 4 bundles, wrap each bundle with kitchen twine and tie securely. Bring a large pot of salted water to a boil, immerse the asparagus bundles (with the tips pointing up) and boil, uncovered, until the asparagus is tender, 6-8 minutes. Remove the bundles and drain for a few seconds, then snip the twine and arrange the asparagus on a warmed platter or plates. Spoon over some of the warm vinaigrette, and pass the rest separately.

Serves 8

GRATIN OF FENNEL AND PARMESAN

This easy gratin is low in fat, making it a good partner for richer main dishes.
Be sure to thoroughly peel the fennel.

4 large fennel bulbs,
ends trimmed

Salt and freshly ground black
pepper, to taste

1½ cups *chicken stock*, preferably
homemade

½ cup freshly grated Parmesan
cheese (2 ounces)

1. Preheat the oven to 400F. With a vegetable peeler, peel the fennel to remove the outer layer of stringy fibers, then cut the bulbs lengthwise in quarters. Arrange the quarters in a shallow baking dish, closely-packed but in a single layer. Pour over the stock (it should come about ⅓ of the way up the fennel), season to taste with salt and pepper, and sprinkle the cheese evenly over the top.

2. Cover the dish with aluminum foil or a lid and bake in the preheated oven for about 25 minutes, then uncover and continue to cook until the fennel is very tender when pierced with a knife, another 20-25 minutes. If the fennel is cooked but the cheese is not yet browned, move the gratin under a heated broiler to brown the cheese. Serve warm or at room temperature.

Serves 8

HARICOT VERT AND LENTIL SAUTE

*A quick toss with lentils, basil and tomatoes turns an ordinary side dish
of green beans into a complement with character!*

¹/2 cup uncooked green lentils

1¹/2 cups *chicken stock,* or water

1¹/2 pounds haricots verts
(French green beans),
ends trimmed

2 medium shallots
(2 ounces), minced

3 tablespoons unsalted butter

1 large *tomato* (12 ounces), *peeled,
seeded* and cut into *dice*

2 tablespoons chopped fresh basil

Salt and freshly ground black
pepper, to taste

1. Combine the lentils and chicken stock in a saucepan, bring to a boil, reduce the
heat and *simmer,* covered, until the lentils are tender, about 30 minutes. (If using
water, season with salt and pepper.) Drain off any unabsorbed stock. (The lentils
may be prepared up to 1 day ahead.)

2. Bring a large pot of salted water to a boil and cook the haricots verts,
uncovered at a rolling boil, until tender, 6-8 minutes. Drain and rinse under very
cold water. (This will help keep the color bright.)

3. In a large sauté pan, cook the shallot in the butter over medium heat until soft
but not brown, about 3 minutes. Add the haricots verts and tomatoes and *sauté*
2-3 minutes, then add the basil and lentils. Season to taste with salt and pepper
and toss until combined and heated through. Serve immediately.

Serves 8

SAVOY CABBAGE AND LEEKS IN CREAM

Witness this cabbage made elegant by association with sweet leeks and a dollop of rich cream—a fine partner for simply roasted meat or poultry.

1 medium head Savoy cabbage (1½ pounds), cored and tough outer leaves discarded

1½ ounces bacon (about 3 slices), cut into ½-inch strips

5 medium *leeks* (2 pounds), white part only, split and cut into ½-inch slices

¾ cup *chicken stock*, preferably homemade

¾ cup heavy cream

Salt and freshly ground black pepper, to taste

Few drops lemon juice

1. Separate the cabbage leaves. Bring a large pot of salted water to a boil and *blanch* the leaves by boiling them for about 2 minutes. Drain, then refresh under cold running water and pat dry with paper towels. Stack several leaves together, roll them up like a cigar and slice crosswise into ¼-inch *chiffonade* strips.

2. In a large saucepan, cook the bacon strips over medium heat until the fat is rendered and the bacon is almost crispy, 3-4 minutes. Drain off most of the fat, leaving 2 tablespoons. Add the sliced leeks to the bacon and *sauté* over medium-high heat, stirring until slightly softened, about 3 minutes.

3. Add the cabbage chiffonade and sauté for another minute, stirring to combine the ingredients. Add the stock, season with salt and pepper, cover and *simmer,* stirring frequently, until the leeks and cabbage are tender, about 20 minutes. Remove the lid, add the cream and simmer uncovered another 10-15 minutes to *reduce* the cream until slightly thickened. (The mixture should be very creamy, but not runny.) Add a few drops of lemon juice, taste and correct seasoning. Serve hot.

Serves 8

MARINATED SLAW

*A sweet-and-sour accent to favorite Southern foods —
try it with our fried chicken or barbecued pork.*

1 head white cabbage (2 pounds),
tough outer leaves removed, cored
and sliced very thinly

3/4 cup finely chopped onion
(1 small onion)

1 cup granulated sugar

1 cup white wine vinegar

3/4 cup oil (such as canola,
safflower, soy)

1 tablespoon dry mustard

1 tablespoon celery seed

1 teaspoon salt

1. In a large dish (not aluminum), layer the cabbage, onion and all but 2 tablespoons of the sugar in several alternating layers, ending with the onion.

2. In a saucepan, combine the remaining ingredients and bring to a boil. Pour the hot dressing over the cabbage mixture. Cover and chill the slaw for at least 24 hours. Toss once or twice during this time, and again just before serving to thoroughly distribute the dressing. Serve cold or at room temperature.

Serves 8

PARSNIP PUREE

*Russet potatoes blend well with sweet parsnips in this satisfying side dish,
though any variety of potato will do.*

2 pounds parsnips, peeled and cut
into large chunks

12 ounces potatoes, peeled and cut
into large chunks

6 tablespoons unsalted butter

1/4 - 1/2 cup warm milk

Pinch freshly grated nutmeg

Salt and freshly ground black
pepper, to taste

1. Place the parsnip and potato chunks in a large pan, cover with cold salted water, bring to a boil and boil until very tender when pierced with a knife, about 20 minutes. Drain thoroughly in a colander.

2. While still hot, pass the parsnips and potatoes through a food mill or ricer into a large bowl (the vegetables may be pureed using an electric mixer also, but do not use a food processor). Add the butter and stir until melted, then stir in the milk, a little at a time, until the puree reaches the desired consistency. Season to taste with the nutmeg, salt and pepper. Serve hot.

Serves 8

COTTON ONION RINGS

"Cotton" simply refers to the way the finely cut onion circles puff up when fried.

2 large red onions (2 pounds), sliced into very thin rings

2 cups buttermilk

Oil (such as canola, safflower or soy), for deep-frying

2 cups all-purpose flour, seasoned to taste with paprika, salt and cayenne pepper

1. Combine the onion rings and buttermilk in a large bowl, cover with plastic wrap and marinate for 30 minutes. Drain the onion rings thoroughly in a colander or strainer (discard the buttermilk).

2. Fill a deep-fryer or large pot with oil to no more than half-full and heat to 375F (use a thermometer). Put the seasoned flour on a large plate or tray and dredge the onion rings to coat lightly.

3. Fry the onion rings a few at a time, stirring gently to prevent their sticking together. (Use the thermometer to help keep the temperature constant.) Fry the rings until they are golden brown, about 3 minutes. Drain for a few moments on paper towels and serve hot.

Serves 8

CORN PUDDING

This silky-textured pudding pairs deliciously with many meat and poultry dishes, especially country ham. For a variation, spike it by adding a few tablespoons of diced green chilies to the batter.

4 eggs

2¹/₂ cups milk

²/₃ cup heavy cream

1 tablespoon granulated sugar

1¹/₂ teaspoons salt

¹/₈ teaspoon nutmeg

¹/₈ teaspoon white pepper

2¹/₂ cups (12 ounces) corn kernels

¹/₂ cup fresh white bread crumbs

3 tablespoons unsalted butter, melted

1. Preheat the oven to 350F. Butter a 2-quart ovenproof dish. Put the eggs, milk, cream, sugar, salt, nutmeg and pepper in a large bowl and whisk until thoroughly combined. Stir in the corn kernels.

2. Pour the custard into the buttered dish. Sprinkle the bread crumbs over the top and drizzle with the melted butter. Place the dish into a **water bath** and bake in the preheated oven until the pudding is firm (but still slightly wobbly in the center) and a skewer inserted into the center comes out clean, about 60 minutes. Remove from the water bath and cool for a few minutes before serving.

Serves 8

CHEVRE SOUFFLE

*Creamy and snow-white, our chevre comes fresh from Brier Run Farm,
a West Virginia producer. Its delicate flavor is showcased in this soufflé.*

**8 tablespoons (1 stick)
unsalted butter**

3/4 cup all-purpose flour

2 cups milk

**6 ounces fresh *chevre* cheese,
cut in pieces**

6 egg yolks

**Salt and freshly ground black
pepper, to taste**

8 egg whites

Pinch dried thyme

1. Preheat the oven to 400F. Butter the inside of a 2½-quart soufflé dish. In a large saucepan, melt the butter, add the flour and whisk to form a smooth **roux**. Cook over medium heat, stirring constantly, for 2-3 minutes. Add the milk and whisk vigorously until the mixture is smooth and thick, then cook at a low boil, stirring continuously, for another 2-3 minutes.

2. Remove the mixture from the heat, add the chevre and stir until the cheese is melted and well-incorporated. Stir in the egg yolks and season generously with salt and pepper (the seasoning should be intense here to compensate for the later addition of the egg whites).

3. With an electric mixer or by hand with a whisk, whip the egg whites until they form soft peaks. Stir ¼ of the egg whites into the cheese mixture to lighten it, then carefully fold in the remaining egg whites. Fill the prepared soufflé mold; it should be about ¾ full. Sprinkle the top of the soufflé with the dried thyme. Bake in the preheated oven until risen, golden brown and just barely firm in the center, 40-45 minutes. Serve immediately.

Serves 8

MUSHROOM SPATZLE

A traditional accompaniment to many game dishes, but delicious with other meats, too.
The mushrooms and onions must be chopped very finely and cooked until they are completely dry.

12 ounces common mushrooms,
minced very finely (2 cups)

1/4 cup very finely minced onion

2 tablespoons unsalted butter

1 1/2 cups all-purpose flour

3 eggs

3 tablespoons milk

Pinch freshly grated nutmeg

Salt and freshly ground black
pepper, to taste

1. In a medium sauté pan, cook the chopped mushrooms and onion in the butter over medium heat until all the mushroom liquid has been rendered and evaporated, about 6 minutes. (The mixture should resemble a coarse paste.) Remove from the heat and cool thoroughly.

2. Put the flour in a medium bowl and make a well in the center. Add the eggs to the well and beat lightly with a fork until mixed. Add the milk, then begin stirring in the center of the bowl, drawing in the flour a little at a time to form a smooth thick batter. Stir in the cooled mushrooms and incorporate well. Season with nutmeg, salt and pepper to taste.

3. Bring a large pot of salted water to a boil. Press the batter through a *spatzle press* or a metal colander so it drops into the boiling water. Alternatively, fit a pastry bag with a small plain tip and fill with the batter. Squeeze out 1-inch lengths, cutting them off with a knife into the water. The spatzle will first sink to the bottom, then rise to the surface of the water when cooked, about 2 minutes. Drain the spatzle thoroughly, toss with a little butter and serve immediately in a warmed bowl. The spatzle may also be drained, then sautéed in butter for a slightly crispy texture.

Serves 8

SAUTEED PARMESAN POLENTA

A golden-crusted accompaniment to fish, poultry and meat — or serve it alone,
topped with your favorite tomato-based pasta sauce.

4¹/2 cups water

1 teaspoon salt

1¹/2 cups coarsely ground
cornmeal (yellow or white)

4 tablespoons (¹/2 stick)
unsalted butter

¹/2 cup freshly grated Parmesan
cheese (2 ounces)

Pinch cayenne pepper

Flour, for dredging

Clarified butter or olive oil,
for frying

1. In a large saucepan, bring 3 cups of the water to a boil with the salt. In a small bowl, combine the cornmeal and the remaining water and stir until smooth. Add the wet cornmeal to the simmering water, stirring quickly to prevent lumps. Reduce the heat and cook at a very low *simmer,* stirring frequently, until the mixture is thick and the cornmeal is no longer gritty, 20-25 minutes.

2. Stir in the butter, grated cheese and cayenne. Taste and correct seasoning. (The polenta may be served at this stage, spooned or piped onto plates as a puree.)

3. Spread the polenta in a ³/4-inch layer in a shallow pan and leave at room temperature to cool and set up. When the polenta is firm, cut out shapes (squares, diamonds, rounds etc.) with a knife or a *pastry cutter.* Dredge the shapes lightly with flour. Heat some butter or olive oil in a heavy-bottomed frying pan and *sauté* the polenta shapes over medium heat until golden brown, about 4 minutes on each side. Serve hot.

Serves 8

Breads

CORN BREAD

*A square of warm golden corn bread is welcome at any meal —
we serve corn bread to every dinner guest.
Our version benefits from the slight tang of buttermilk.*

2 eggs

1/3 cup granulated sugar

4 tablespoons (1/2 stick) unsalted
butter, melted

2 cups all-purpose flour

1 1/4 cups corn meal

2 tablespoons baking powder

1 tablespoon salt

2 cups buttermilk

1. Preheat the oven to 425F. Grease a 10-inch square pan. Combine the eggs, sugar and melted butter in a medium bowl and beat with an electric mixer or a wooden spoon until mixed.

2. Sift together the flour, corn meal, baking powder and salt, add to the egg mixture and stir until just combined. Add the buttermilk and stir until smooth. Pour the batter into the prepared pan and bake in the preheated oven until golden brown and a skewer inserted into the center comes out clean, 25-30 minutes. Cool partially, then cut into squares. Serve warm or at room temperature.

Makes 16 2 1/2-inch squares

Pictured on page 150: Corn Bread, Dorothy's Popovers, Zucchini Bread

DOROTHY'S POPOVERS

Dorothy Draper served popovers at most of her meals.
Golden and crisp on the outside, with a moist eggy center,
these popovers will disappear from the table fast!

2 eggs

1 1/2 cups milk

2 teaspoons unsalted butter, melted

1/2 teaspoon salt

3/4 cup plus 1 tablespoon all-purpose flour

Generous pinch dried thyme

1. Preheat the oven to 375F. Grease a muffin tin that makes 12 small muffins. In a medium bowl, combine the eggs, milk, melted butter and salt and mix well with an electric mixer or a whisk.

2. Put the flour in another bowl and make a well in the center. Pour in the milk mixture gradually, whisking until smooth.

3. Pour the batter into the prepared muffin tin, filling the cups 3/4 full. Sprinkle each popover with a tiny pinch of thyme. Bake in the preheated oven until puffed high and golden brown, about 30 minutes. Serve immediately.

Makes about 1 dozen small popovers

ZUCCHINI BREAD

This quick bread is not too sweet —delicious on its own or paired with savory foods.
Be sure to use very fresh oil.

3 cups all-purpose flour

4 teaspoons cinnamon

2¹/2 teaspoons baking powder

1 teaspoon baking soda

¹/2 teaspoon salt

4 eggs

1¹/2 cups granulated sugar

1 cup oil (such as canola,
sunflower or safflower)

1 tablespoon vanilla extract

2¹/2 cups grated zucchini
(1 pound zucchini)

1. Preheat the oven to 375F. Grease and flour 2 8¹/2 x 4¹/2-inch loaf pans. Sift together the flour, cinnamon, baking powder, baking soda and salt.

2. In a large bowl with an electric mixer or a wooden spoon, beat the eggs and sugar together until well mixed. Add the oil and vanilla and beat until combined. Stir in the grated zucchini, then add the dry ingredients and stir until just combined; do not overmix.

3. Pour the batter into the prepared loaf pans and bake in the preheated oven until a skewer inserted into the center comes out clean, about 45 minutes. Cool on a rack before slicing.

Makes 2 8¹/2 x 4¹/2-inch loaves

PECAN BREAD

A moist nutty bread to serve for brunch or tea.

3 cups all-purpose flour	2 cups granulated sugar
1¹/₂ teaspoons baking powder	5 eggs
¹/₄ teaspoon salt	1 cup evaporated milk
16 tablespoons (2 sticks) unsalted butter, softened at room temperature	1 teaspoon vanilla extract
	1¹/₂ cups chopped pecans

1. Preheat the oven to 350F. Grease and flour a 9-inch tube or bundt pan. Sift together the flour, baking powder and salt.

2. With an electric mixer or a wooden spoon, cream the butter and sugar in a large bowl until very light and fluffy. Add the eggs 1 at a time, beating after each addition until well mixed.

3. Blend in the dry ingredients and the milk, in 3 alternating batches, working the batter only until just combined. Stir in the vanilla and the nuts.

4. Pour the batter into the prepared pan and bake in the preheated oven until a skewer inserted into the center comes out clean, 50-55 minutes. Cool on a rack for a few minutes, then unmold the cake onto the rack and cool completely.

Makes 1 9-inch tube-shaped loaf

PUMPKIN MUFFINS

These moist spicy muffins are one of the many house-baked breads we offer at breakfast, and one of our most requested recipes—a great way to start the day!

8 tablespoons (1 stick) unsalted butter, softened at room temperature

1 cup granulated sugar

1¼ cups canned pumpkin

2 eggs

2 cups all-purpose flour

2 teaspoons baking powder

1½ teaspoons cinnamon

½ teaspoon nutmeg

¼ teaspoon salt

1 cup milk

½ cup chopped pecans or walnuts

½ cup raisins

1 tablespoon cinnamon-sugar, for sprinkling

1. Preheat the oven to 375F. Grease the muffin pan or use a non-stick pan. With an electric mixer or a wooden spoon, cream the butter and sugar together until smooth and fluffy. Add the pumpkin and mix until well-blended, then add the eggs 1 at a time, stirring until completely mixed after each addition.

2. Sift together the flour, baking powder, cinnamon, nutmeg and salt. Stir into the pumpkin mixture, alternating with the milk. Stir just enough to combine the ingredients; do not overmix. Fold in the nuts and raisins.

3. Pour the batter into the prepared muffin pan, filling the cups ²/₃ full. Sprinkle on a little cinnamon sugar. Bake in the preheated oven until a skewer inserted into the center comes out clean, about 25 minutes. Remove from the pan and cool on a rack. Serve for breakfast or tea. (The muffins may be stored up to 2 days in an airtight container or frozen up to 1 month.)

Makes 2 dozen small muffins

GREENBRIER BUTTERMILK BISCUITS

Nothing says Southern cooking as well as buttermilk biscuits.
Our version is light and tender, a perfect pocket for a thin slice of Smithfield ham.

3¹/4 cups all-purpose flour	7 teaspoons baking powder
1 tablespoon salt	³/4 cup shortening
1¹/2 teaspoons granulated sugar	1³/4 - 2 cups buttermilk

1. Preheat the oven to 425F. Grease a baking sheet. Sift all the dry ingredients together in a large bowl. With your fingers or a **pastry blender,** cut or rub the shortening into the dry ingredients until the texture resembles coarse meal. Add 1³/4 cups of the buttermilk and stir until the ingredients are just combined. (The dough should be very soft but not sticky. If too dry, add more buttermilk.)

2. Turn the dough out onto a lightly floured work surface and knead lightly by folding it over on itself 3 to 4 times. Roll or pat the dough into a ³/4-inch layer. With a round **pastry cutter,** cut out the biscuits and transfer them to the prepared baking sheet. Lightly knead the scraps together, pat into an even layer and cut out more biscuits. (Cut the biscuits to produce the minimum of scraps because the more the dough is worked, the less tender those biscuits will be.) Discard any scraps remaining after the second cut.

3. Bake in the preheated oven until risen and golden brown on the top and bottom, 10-12 minutes for the large biscuits, 8-10 for the small size. Serve hot or at room temperature.

Makes 20 2-inch or 30 1-inch biscuits

FRUIT-STUDDED SCONES

*The next-best thing to afternoon tea at Draper's Cafe
is a batch of these scones at home.*

1³/4 cups all-purpose flour

2 tablespoons granulated sugar

4 teaspoons baking powder

¹/4 teaspoon salt

4 tablespoons (¹/2 stick)
unsalted butter, cut in pieces

¹/4 cup mixed candied fruit
(cherries, apricots, pineapple),
very finely chopped

2 tablespoons dried currants

³/4 cup milk

1. Preheat the oven to 400F. Grease a baking sheet. In a medium bowl sift together the flour, sugar, baking powder and salt. With a ***pastry blender*** or your fingers, cut or rub the butter into the dry ingredients until the texture resembles coarse meal. Add the fruit and currants.

2. Add the milk and stir just until the mixture forms a soft dough, adding a little more flour if the dough is too sticky. Place the dough on a lightly floured work surface and roll out to a layer ³/4 inch thick. Cut out 2-inch circles with a ***pastry cutter*** and place the scones on the baking sheet about ¹/2 inch apart. (Knead the scraps together lightly and reroll once for the last few scones.) Bake in the preheated oven until risen and firm to the touch (the scones should remain fairly pale), about 10 minutes. Serve at room temperature with Devonshire cream and strawberry preserves or butter.

Makes about 2 dozen 2-inch scones

Desserts

THE TAVERN APPLE PIE

An all-American favorite, the version we serve in our Tavern Room and Draper's is piled high with tart juicy apples.

For the crust:

2 cups all-purpose flour

8 tablespoons (1 stick) cold unsalted butter, cut in pieces

1 teaspoon salt

1 egg yolk

2 - 4 tablespoons cold water

8 medium Golden Delicious apples, peeled, cored and sliced in 1/4-inch slices

1 cup granulated sugar

2 tablespoons all-purpose flour

2 tablespoons unsalted butter, cut in small bits

1/2 teaspoon cinnamon

1/4 teaspoon nutmeg

Juice from 1/2 lemon

Granulated sugar, for sprinkling

1. Preheat the oven to 375F. Make the crust: combine the flour, butter and salt in a food processor and, using the pulse button, process until the mixture has the texture of coarse meal. With the motor running, add the yolk and just enough of the water for the dough to begin to form a loose ball. Transfer the dough to a lightly floured work surface and shape with your hands into a smooth ball. Cover with plastic wrap and chill for at least 20 minutes. Divide the chilled dough into 2 pieces, 1 slightly larger than the other (to use for the top crust).

2. On a lightly floured work surface, roll out the smaller piece of dough to form a circle 14 inches in diameter and 1/8 inch thick. Lift the dough by rolling it loosely around the rolling pin and transfer it to a 10-inch pie pan. Line the pan evenly with the dough, leaving the excess hanging over the edge.

3. In a large bowl, toss the apple slices with all remaining ingredients (except the sprinkling sugar) until combined. Mound the apples on the unbaked pie crust (they will rise several inches above the edge of the pan). Roll out the larger piece of dough to a circle 18 inches in diameter and 1/8 inch thick and drape it over the mounded apples, pressing lightly with your hands so it conforms to the shape of the apples. Press the 2 layers of pastry together at the edge. Trim off any excess dough. Crimp the sealed edge with your fingers or a fork to seal. Sprinkle the surface with a little sugar, if desired. With a sharp knife, poke several slits in the top of the crust in a decorative pattern to release steam during cooking.

4. Bake the pie in the preheated oven until the pastry is an even golden brown, about 45 minutes. Serve warm or at room temperature.

Makes 1 10-inch pie

Pictured on page 160: The Tavern Apple Pie, Cashew Pie, Lemon Chess Tart

LEMON CHESS TART

A slice of this bright and sunny Southern favorite makes a perfect end to any meal.

For the crust:

1 cup all-purpose flour

4 tablespoons (1/2 stick) cold unsalted butter, cut in pieces

1/2 teaspoon salt

1 egg yolk

1-3 tablespoons cold water

5 eggs

1 1/4 cups granulated sugar

1 1/2 tablespoons all-purpose flour

1 1/2 tablespoons cornmeal

1/4 cup milk

1/2 cup lemon juice

Grated *zest* from 2 lemons

3 tablespoons unsalted butter, melted

1. Make the pie pastry: in a food processor, combine the flour, butter and salt and process using the pulse button until the mixture has the texture of coarse meal. With the motor running, add the yolk and just enough of the water for the dough to begin to form a loose ball. Transfer the dough to a lightly floured work surface and shape into a smooth ball. Cover the dough with plastic wrap and chill for at least 20 minutes.

2. Preheat the oven to 375F. Roll out the dough on a lightly floured work surface to a circle 13 inches in diameter and 1/8 inch thick. Lift the dough by rolling it loosely around the rolling pin and gently lay it in the tart pan, pressing well into the corners. Trim off the excess crust and crimp the edges with your fingers or a fork for a decorative finish. **Blind-bake** the crust in the preheated oven until it is partially baked, about 12 minutes. Remove from the oven and cool slightly. Reduce the oven temperature to 350F.

3. With an electric mixer or by hand, beat together the eggs and sugar in a medium bowl until combined (do not beat vigorously; the mixture should not be fluffy). Add the flour, cornmeal, milk, lemon juice, lemon zest and melted butter in that order, beating a few seconds between each addition. Continue to beat for 5 minutes at medium speed (or longer if mixing by hand). Pour the filling into the partially baked crust and return to the oven. Bake until the filling is barely firm and light golden brown on top, 25-35 minutes. Cool before serving.

Makes 1 10-inch tart

CASHEW PIE

The Greenbrier's twist on traditional Southern pecan pie.

For the crust:

1 cup all-purpose flour

4 tablespoons (1/2 stick) cold unsalted butter, cut in pieces

1/2 teaspoon salt

1 egg yolk

1-3 tablespoons cold water

3 eggs

3/4 cup granulated sugar

3/4 cup dark corn syrup

3/4 cup light corn syrup

1 teaspoon vanilla extract

1/4 teaspoon salt

2 tablespoons unsalted butter, melted

2 cups (10 ounces) roasted cashew halves or pieces

1. Preheat the oven to 375F. Make the crust: in a food processor, combine the flour, butter and salt and process using the pulse button until the mixture has the texture of coarse meal. With the motor running, add the yolk and just enough of the water for the dough to begin to form a loose ball. Transfer the dough to a lightly floured work surface and shape into a smooth ball. Cover the dough with plastic wrap and chill for at least 20 minutes.

2. Roll out the dough on a lightly floured work surface to a circle 13 inches in diameter and 1/8 inch thick. Lift the dough by rolling it loosely around the rolling pin and gently lay it in the pie pan, pressing into the corners. Trim off the excess dough and crimp the edges with your fingers or a fork for a decorative finish. **Blind-bake** the crust in the preheated oven until it is partially baked, about 12 minutes. Remove from the oven and cool slightly. Reduce the oven temperature to 350F.

3. Combine the eggs, sugar, syrups, vanilla and salt in a medium bowl and beat with an electric mixer (or by hand with a whisk) until thoroughly blended, about 2 minutes, then beat in the melted butter. Fill the partially-baked crust with the cashews, then pour in the syrup mixture. Bake in the preheated oven until the pie is deep golden brown and no longer feels liquid in the center, about 45 minutes. Cool before cutting into slices.

Makes 1 9-inch pie

PUMPKIN CAKE CHANTILLY

*This not-too-sweet layer cake makes a nice change of pace from
more traditional flavors. Be sure to use very fresh oil.*

4 eggs

2 cups granulated sugar

1 cup oil (such as canola,
safflower or soy)

2 cups canned pumpkin

2 cups cake flour

2 teaspoons baking powder

1 teaspoon salt

2 teaspoons cinnamon

2 cups heavy cream

1/4 cup confectioner's sugar

1 teaspoon vanilla extract

1 tablespoon rum or brandy

1/2 cup graham cracker crumbs or
finely chopped nuts

1. Preheat the oven to 325F. Grease and flour 2 8-inch round cake pans. With an
electric mixer, beat together the eggs and sugar in a large bowl until light and pale
yellow. Add the oil and beat until well mixed. Add the pumpkin and beat until
smooth.

2. Sift together the dry ingredients then add them to the pumpkin mixture and
beat until just blended (do not overbeat). Pour the batter into the prepared pans
and bake in the preheated oven until a skewer inserted into the center comes out
clean, 35-40 minutes. Cool the cakes a few minutes in the pan, then invert them
on a cake rack to cool completely.

3. Whip the cream until slightly thick. Add the confectioner's sugar, vanilla and
rum and continue to whip until the cream forms soft peaks. Spread 1/4 of the
whipped cream on the surface of 1 cake, then top it with the other cake. Frost the
top and sides of the cake with the remaining cream. Gently pat the graham
cracker crumbs or chopped nuts around the sides to decorate. Keep refrigerated
until ready to serve.

Makes 1 8-inch layer cake

CLASSIC CHEESECAKE

*This slightly dense but extremely creamy cake is truly a classic
and the perfect foil for a colorful fresh fruit topping.*

1¼ cups graham cracker crumbs

1¾ cups granulated sugar

8 tablespoons (1 stick) unsalted
butter, melted

3 pounds cream cheese, softened
at room temperature

3 tablespoons lemon juice

1 tablespoon grated lemon *zest*

1 tablespoon vanilla extract

Pinch salt

6 eggs

1. Preheat the oven to 375F. Mix the graham cracker crumbs, ¼ cup of the sugar and melted butter together and press into an even layer on the bottom and sides of a 10-inch springform pan. (Don't worry if the sides aren't perfectly covered.) Bake in the preheated oven until slightly toasted, about 5 minutes. Remove from the oven and cool. Reduce the oven temperature to 300F.

2. With an electric mixer, cream together the softened cream cheese and remaining sugar. Add the lemon juice, lemon zest, vanilla and salt, then add the eggs 1 at a time, beating well after each addition. Pour the batter into the cooled crust and bake in the preheated oven until the center of the cake is no longer wobbly, about 1½ hours.

3. When the cake is cooked, turn off the oven, partially open the oven door and let the cake cool for 2 hours before removing. (The gradual reduction in temperature will help prevent cracking.) Remove the cake from the oven and cool completely at room temperature. Run a sharp knife around the inside of the springform to loosen the cake, then remove the ring and transfer the cake to a serving plate. Serve plain or topped with fresh fruit compote.

Makes 1 10-inch cheesecake

SOUR CHERRY AND PEACH GINGER CRISPS

Almost any mix of fruit would be delicious in this comforting dessert.
The crunchy topping gets a little kick from candied ginger.

1 1/2 pounds pitted fresh sour cherries or well-drained canned sour cherries

1 pound well-drained *diced Greenbrier peaches* or peeled, pitted and diced fresh ripe peaches

1/2 cup granulated sugar

1 1/2 cups all-purpose flour

1 1/4 cups brown sugar, packed

12 tablespoons (1 1/2 sticks) unsalted butter, softened at room temperature

1 cup rolled oats

2 tablespoons finely chopped crystallized ginger

1. Preheat the oven to 375F. Combine the fruit in a strainer or colander and drain again for 15-20 minutes. Butter 8 1-cup ramekins or a 2-quart baking dish. In a medium bowl, toss the drained fruit with the granulated sugar and 5 tablespoons of the flour; distribute evenly in the ramekins or the dish.

2. With an electric mixer or by hand with a wooden spoon, cream together the brown sugar and butter until just combined. Add the remaining flour, oatmeal and ginger and stir just until the ingredients are incorporated (the mixture should be slightly lumpy).

3. Crumble the topping mixture in an even layer over the fruit and bake in the preheated oven until the topping is bubbly and brown, 12-15 minutes for the individual ramekins, 15-18 for the larger dish. Remove the crisps from the oven and cool slightly before serving.

Serves 8

MIXED BERRY GRATIN WITH FRAMBOISE SABAYON

A light cloak of this sabayon lets the bright flavors of the berries shine through.
Be patient and cook the egg yolks over very gentle heat to get the correct consistency.

**2 pounds fresh mixed berries
(such as raspberries, strawberries,
blackberries, blueberries),
rinsed and trimmed as necessary**

6 egg yolks

6 tablespoons granulated sugar

**¹/₃ cup framboise
(raspberry brandy)**

1 cup heavy cream

1. Dry the berries thoroughly and arrange in a shallow oven-proof serving dish or individual dishes.

2. In the top of a ***double boiler***, whisk together the yolks, sugar and framboise. Over simmering but not boiling water, whisk the mixture vigorously and constantly until it is thick, pale yellow and tripled in volume (the bottom of the bowl should never be too hot to touch with your bare hand), for about 8 minutes. (A hand-held electric mixer will make this job easier.) Remove the sabayon from the heat and leave to cool slightly.

3. Preheat the broiler. Whip the cream until it forms soft peaks, then gently fold into the sabayon. Spoon an even layer over the fruit and broil until golden brown, about 2 minutes, turning the plate as necessary for an even color. Serve immediately.

Serves 8

FROZEN GRAND MARNIER MOUSSE IN ALMOND LACE COOKIE CUPS

This elegant frozen mousse has the texture of light ice cream, yet requires no time-consuming churning. Serve it on its own or framed in a crisp almond cookie cup.

6 egg yolks	Grated *zest* of 1 orange
1/2 cup granulated sugar	2 cups heavy cream
2 tablespoons Grand Marnier (or other orange liqueur)	2 tablespoons *blanched julienne* of orange zest
2 tablespoons fresh orange juice	8 sprigs fresh mint

1. Combine the egg yolks, sugar, Grand Marnier and orange juice in the top of a **double boiler** and whisk to combine. Place the pan over simmering but not boiling water and continue to whisk constantly (the bottom of the bowl should never be too hot to touch) until the mixture is very thick and fluffy and has tripled in volume, about 8 minutes. (A hand-held electric mixer makes this an easier job.) Fold in the grated orange zest, then cool slightly.

2. Whip the cream until it forms soft peaks. Gently fold the whipped cream into the egg yolk mixture until well-blended. Pour the mousse into a bowl, cover and freeze at least 12 hours. Remove the mousse from the freezer about 15 minutes before serving to soften it slightly. Put 1 scoop of mousse in each cookie cup, top with a little blanched zest and a sprig of mint.

Serves 8

Almond Lace Cookie Cups

Shaping these delicate cookies into cups can be slightly tricky. If the cookies become too stiff to shape, return them to the warm oven for a few seconds to soften.

¹/₃ cup dark brown sugar, packed

4 tablespoons (¹/₂ stick) unsalted butter

¹/₄ cup light corn syrup

1 teaspoon grated orange *zest*

¹/₃ cup cake flour

¹/₂ cup chopped almonds

1. Preheat the oven to 350F. Thoroughly grease a baking sheet. In a small saucepan, combine the sugar, butter, corn syrup and orange zest. Cook over low heat until the butter and sugar are melted. Remove from the heat and stir in the flour and nuts.

2. Spoon 1 scant tablespoon of batter for each cookie onto the prepared sheet, spacing them far apart to allow for spreading (only 2 - 3 cookies per sheet). Bake in the preheated oven until the cookies are golden brown and bubbly, 6 - 8 minutes.

3. Remove the pan from the oven and cool the cookies for 1 - 2 minutes, then loosen them with a spatula. With your hand, immediately transfer each cookie to an inverted coffee cup or glass and mold the cookie into a cup shape. After a couple of minutes, transfer the cookie cups to a rack to cool completely. (The cookies may be prepared up to 2 days ahead and stored in an airtight container.)

Makes 12 cookies

GREENBRIER "DALEY" BREAD PUDDING WITH VANILLA SAUCE AND PEACH COULIS

This Greenbrier favorite tastes even better when made with our special cinnamon "Daley" bread, developed from a recipe offered by a long-time guest of the same name.

1 1-pound loaf Greenbrier Daley bread (or other good-quality cinnamon raisin bread)	4 cups milk
	1 cup granulated sugar
	1/2 cup raisins
8 tablespoons (1 stick) unsalted butter, melted	1 tablespoon vanilla extract
6 eggs	1 1/2 teaspoons cinnamon

1. Preheat the oven to 375F. Cut the bread into 1-inch squares, spread on a baking sheet and toast in the preheated oven until light brown, about 8 minutes. Pack the toasted bread into a 2 1/2-quart baking dish or into 8 1-cup ramekins and drizzle with the melted butter.

2. In a medium bowl, whisk together the eggs, milk and sugar until the sugar is dissolved. Add the raisins, vanilla and cinnamon. Pour the custard over the bread and leave to soak about 10 minutes. Reduce the oven temperature to 350F. Bake the pudding in the preheated oven until slightly puffed and firm, about 45 minutes. Cool slightly and serve warm with vanilla sauce and peach coulis.

Serves 8

Vanilla Sauce

1 cup heavy cream	1 1/2 teaspoons vanilla extract
1/4 cup granulated sugar	1/8 teaspoon salt
2 egg yolks	1 medium scoop vanilla ice cream
1 1/2 teaspoons all-purpose flour	

1. In a small saucepan, combine the cream and sugar and bring to a boil, stirring to dissolve the sugar. In a small bowl, whisk together the egg yolks, flour, vanilla and salt until smooth and pale yellow.

2. Pour a little of the hot cream into the yolk mixture, whisking rapidly until smooth, then pour all of the yolk mixture back into the pan of cream. Cook over very low heat (do not boil), stirring constantly with a wooden spoon, until the cream has thickened slightly. (To test, run your finger across the back of the cream-coated spoon; if it leaves a clear trace, the sauce is ready.) Remove from the heat, stir in the scoop of ice cream until melted and strain the sauce through a fine sieve. Serve warm or at room temperature.

Makes 1 1/2 cups

Peach Coulis

3 *Greenbrier peach* halves, drained
1/2 cup puree from Greenbrier
    peaches

1 tablespoon lemon juice

1. Combine the ingredients in a blender and work until the ***coulis*** is very smooth and pourable, adding a little water if necessary to get the right consistency.

Makes 1 1/2 cups

DARK CHOCOLATE POTS DE CREME

*These little custards are deeply chocolate and satiny smooth, tempting alone or
with a dollop of whipped cream.*

3 cups heavy cream

4 ounces good-quality semi-sweet
chocolate, chopped

1 teaspoon kirsch or other brandy

7 egg yolks

1/2 cup granulated sugar

1. Preheat the oven to 350F. Combine the cream, chopped chocolate and kirsch in
the top of a *double boiler* and heat, stirring, until the chocolate is melted and the
ingredients are well blended.

2. In a medium bowl, combine the egg yolks and sugar and whisk until combined
(do not whisk vigorously; the mixture should not be frothy).

3. Pour a little of the hot chocolate mixture into the eggs and stir well, then add
the rest and stir to combine. Strain through a fine sieve into 8 4-ounce ramekins
set in a *water bath.* Lay a sheet of buttered wax paper on top of the ramekins.
Bake the custards in the preheated oven until they are no longer liquid but still
slightly wobbly in the center, 20 - 25 minutes. Cool before serving.

Makes 8 4-ounce servings

CHOCOLATE SOUFFLE PUDDING

Half airy soufflé, half moist pudding, this dessert is designed for true chocolate lovers.
Try it with a drizzle of vanilla sauce (page 172) or heavy cream.

5 eggs, separated

3/4 cup granulated sugar

1/2 cup all-purpose flour

2 cups milk

8 tablespoons (1 stick)
unsalted butter

1 teaspoon vanilla extract

2 ounces semi-sweet
chocolate, melted

1. Preheat the oven to 350F. Butter the inside of a 2 1/2-quart soufflé dish and sprinkle with a little sugar, shaking off any excess. In a small bowl with a whisk or electric mixer, beat together the egg yolks and 1/2 the sugar until thick and pale yellow, then beat in the flour.

2. In a large saucepan, bring the milk, butter, and vanilla to a boil. Pour a little of the hot milk into the yolk mixture and whisk until very smooth. Pour all the mixture back into the pan of milk and continue cooking over low heat, whisking constantly, until thick and just starting to boil. Remove from the heat, add the melted chocolate and stir to combine thoroughly.

3. With an electric mixer or by hand with a whisk, beat the egg whites in a large bowl until foamy, then add the remaining sugar bit by bit, beating constantly until the mixture forms a glossy meringue that holds soft peaks. Stir 1/4 of the meringue into the chocolate mixture to loosen it, then carefully fold in the rest.

4. Pour the soufflé mixture into the prepared soufflé dish. Bake in the preheated oven until risen and just barely firm in the center, about 30 minutes. Serve immediately.

Serves 8

DOUBLE CHOCOLATE PATE

This dessert is a slice of paradise for the chocoholic, with its velvety chocolate center enrobed in crisp chocolate couverture.

8 ounces good-quality semi-sweet chocolate, roughly chopped

4 egg yolks

1/2 cup granulated sugar

4 tablespoons cognac (or liqueur such as Grand Marnier)

2 cups heavy cream

For the chocolate coating:

8 ounces good-quality semi-sweet chocolate, roughly chopped

3 tablespoons unsalted butter

1/2 cup heavy cream

1. Cut a piece of plastic wrap 15 inches long and 10 inches wide (or the length of the loaf pan). Line the pan with the plastic, keeping it as smooth as possible, so the 2 long sides and the bottom are covered but the 2 short sides stay bare (greasing the inside of the pan will help stick the plastic in place). Put the chopped chocolate in a ***double boiler*** and melt over low heat. Cool slightly.

2. In another double boiler, combine the egg yolks, sugar and cognac and whisk constantly over simmering but not boiling water (the bottom of the bowl should never be too hot to touch) until the mixture is very thick and fluffy and has tripled in volume, about 5 minutes. Remove from the heat and fold in the melted chocolate. (The mixture may appear stiff at this stage.)

3. Whip the cream in a large bowl until it forms soft peaks. Stir a small amount of the whipped cream into the chocolate mixture; repeat until the mixture is fairly loose and the chocolate is well-blended with the cream, then fold in the remaining whipped cream. Pour the mousse into the prepared loaf pan, rapping the pan lightly on the work surface to eliminate any air bubbles. Fold the plastic wrap securely over the top of the pan and freeze the pâté for at least 24 hours.

4. The next day, make the chocolate coating: melt the chocolate and butter together in a double boiler, then stir in the cream. Cut a piece of heavy cardboard so it fits exactly into the top of the loaf pan; cover it with plastic wrap or aluminum foil. Invert the pâté onto the cardboard and remove the pan and plastic wrap. Place the pâté on a rack with a tray or plate underneath to catch the excess chocolate. Pour the chocolate coating evenly over the pâté, spreading with a spatula if necessary to coat the top surface and sides, and reserving the excess. Return the pâté on the cardboard to the freezer.

5. When the coating is firm, flip the pâté so the uncoated side is up. Reheat the remaining chocolate coating and pour it onto the uncoated surface, smoothing with a spatula. Return the pâté to the freezer until ready to serve. To serve, slice the frozen pâté with a thin-bladed knife into 1/2-inch slices (to make slicing easier, run the knife under hot water, wipe dry, then slice.) Arrange each slice on a dessert plate and let rest 4 - 5 minutes to soften slightly before serving.

Makes 1 10 x 4-inch loaf

AMARETTO TRUFFLES

Rich, bitter chocolate truffles—the perfect ending to an elegant Greenbrier meal.
The Greenbrier Candymaker dips each truffle in tempered chocolate for a crisp coating;
this recipe uses the simpler method of a cocoa powder or nut coating.

12 ounces good-quality semi-sweet chocolate, finely chopped

1 cup heavy cream

1 tablespoon Amaretto liqueur (or try cognac, Grand Marnier, framboise, etc.)

1/2 cup good-quality unsweetened cocoa powder

3/4 cup finely chopped almonds, lightly toasted

1. Put the chocolate in a medium bowl. Bring the cream to a boil and quickly pour it over the chocolate. Let it rest for about 1 minute, then whisk vigorously until the chocolate is completely melted and the mixture is smooth; this is a ganache. Add the Amaretto and whisk again until smooth. Cover the ganache loosely with plastic wrap and leave in the refrigerator until firm, at least 6 hours, preferably overnight.

2. When the ganache is firm, remove from the refrigerator and leave at room temperature about 15 minutes. Put the cocoa in 1 shallow bowl and the chopped nuts in another. With a melon baller or small teaspoon, scoop out a little ganache, and with your hands shape into little balls (they should not be perfectly smooth, as they are meant to resemble real truffles). To make cocoa-coated truffles, drop the balls into the cocoa powder and roll or shake to thoroughly coat with cocoa, then transfer to a tray. For almond-coated truffles, drop the balls into the chopped almonds, roll to coat completely and press lightly to help the almonds adhere. Transfer to a tray. Store the truffles in a tightly covered container in a cool dry place (but not the refrigerator—it is too moist) for up to 1 week. (If the cocoa powder becomes absorbed into the ganache during storage, the truffles may be redusted with more cocoa powder.)

Makes about 3 dozen 1-inch truffles

ALMOND MACAROONS

*Crisp and chewy, these almondy drops are a delight at teatime or
with coffee at the end of an elegant meal.*

½ cup almond paste	¼ cup confectioner's sugar
6 tablespoons granulated sugar	2 egg whites
¼ cup all-purpose flour	Additional sugar, for sprinkling

1. Preheat the oven to 350F. Grease a baking sheet and dust it lightly with flour, shaking off any excess. Combine all the ingredients except the egg whites and additional sugar in a food processor and work until they are well-incorporated into fine granules. Add the egg whites and process until thoroughly combined.

2. Drop the batter onto the prepared baking sheet using a teaspoon or a pastry bag fitted with a plain tip, making small mounds about the diameter of a quarter, spaced 1 inch apart. Sprinkle the cookies with a little sugar. Bake in the preheated oven until light brown, 10 - 12 minutes. With a spatula, remove immediately from the baking sheet and cool on a rack. The macaroons may be stored in an airtight container up to 1 week.

Makes about 3 dozen cookies

Glossary of Basic Recipes, Techniques and Terms

This glossary contains recipes for some basic preparations called for in this book, as well as explanations of many culinary techniques and terms. (All entries are marked in bold italic type the first time they appear in the body of a recipe.) It is not intended to be an exhaustive reference section, addressing only selected subjects mentioned in this book.

BASIC RECIPES

Chicken Stock *(makes approximately 2 quarts)*
1 2 1/2-pound chicken
2 small onions, quartered
2 medium carrots, quartered
2 medium ribs celery, quartered
1 leek, white part only, quartered
1 clove garlic, crushed
10 black peppercorns
1 clove
1 large bouquet garni

1. Place the ingredients in a stock pot and add cold water just to cover. Bring to a simmer and cook 2 - 3 hours, skimming away all the foam and fat that accumulate at the surface. Do not let the stock boil.

2. Strain the stock through a fine sieve. Skim away any visible grease on the surface, then chill several hours and skim again until the stock is fat-free. Refrigerate 3 - 4 days or freeze up to 3 months.

Brown Veal Stock *(makes approximately 2 quarts)*
4 pounds veal bones, preferably knuckle bones
2 small onions, quartered
2 medium carrots, quartered
2 medium ribs celery, quartered
1 leek, white part only, quartered
1 tomato, quartered, or 1 tablespoon tomato paste
1 large bouquet garni
10 black peppercorns

1. Preheat the oven to 450F. Place the bones in a roasting pan and roast in the preheated oven until thoroughly browned, about 30 minutes. (If the bones are completely fat-free, add a tablespoon of oil to the pan before adding the bones.) Add the vegetables and cook another 10-15 minutes until the vegetables are browned also. Transfer the bones and vegetables to a stock pot. Pour off all the grease from the roasting pan and deglaze by dissolving the caramelized juices with some water or wine. Add to the stock pot. Add the tomato, bouquet garni and peppercorns. Add cold water just to cover the bones.

2. Bring to a simmer and cook over low heat 4-5 hours, skimming away all the foam and fat that accumulate on the surface. Do not let the stock boil.

3. Strain the stock through a fine sieve. Skim away any visible grease on the surface, then chill several hours and skim again until the stock is fat-free. Refrigerate 3 - 4 days or freeze up to 3 months.

NOTE: Beef, venison or lamb stock is made in the same manner, but with bones from the appropriate animal.

Fish Stock *(makes approximately 2 quarts)*

1 teaspoon oil (such as olive, canola or soy)
1 large onion, sliced
2¹/2 pounds fish bones, washed well and cut into large pieces
1 cup dry white wine
10 black peppercorns
1 bouquet garni

1. Cook the oil and onion together in a stock pot until the onion is soft but not brown, about 5 minutes. Add the fish bones and continue to cook until the bones whiten and start to render their juices, another 3-5 minutes. Add the wine, simmer for 3-4 minutes, then add the peppercorns, bouquet garni and 2 quarts cold water. Bring to a boil, then immediately reduce the heat to a bare simmer and simmer for 20 minutes (count from the time the stock comes to a boil).

2. Strain the stock through a fine sieve; do not press on the bones. Skim away any visible fat. Refrigerate 2-3 days or freeze up to 3 months.

NOTE ON STOCK ALTERNATIVES: If it is not convenient to make stocks from scratch, there are several acceptable store-bought alternatives. Canned low-salt chicken or beef broth is the best choice, with good-quality bouillon cubes as another possibility. For fish stock, try a mixture of bottled clam juice and water. Most prepared products are quite salty, so adjust the amount of added salt in the recipe to compensate, especially if the stock will be reduced. Glace de viande should be made only from homemade stock.

Quick Puff Pastry (_Makes 1 pound pastry)_
(a modified version of classic puff pastry)

2¹/4 cups all-purpose flour
1 teaspoon salt
16 tablespoons (2 sticks) unsalted butter, cut into ¹/4-inch pieces
¹/2 cup cold water, or more as needed

1. Put the flour, salt and ¹/2 of the butter into a food processor and work, using the pulse button, until the mixture resembles coarse meal. With the motor running, pour in the water, a little at a time, and work just until the dough begins to form a rough ball. Do not overwork. Transfer the dough to a lightly floured work surface and shape into a smooth ball. Wrap in plastic and chill for about 15 minutes.

2. On a lightly floured surface, roll out the dough to a rectangle 8 inches by 16 inches. Arrange the remaining pieces of butter in an even layer over ²/3 of the length of the rectangle. Fold the unbuttered ¹/3 over the dough, then fold again (like a business letter) so the butter is completely wrapped in dough. Press lightly to seal, wrap in plastic and chill again for a few minutes.

3. Unwrap it and roll out the dough packet until it again forms a large rectangle, positioned vertically on the work surface before you. Fold in thirds as before, press to seal, rotate the dough 90 degrees so it again is positioned vertically. Roll out to a rectangle once more, fold in thirds, and press. Wrap the dough and chill for 20-30 minutes. The dough is now ready to roll out and use in your recipe as directed.

TECHNIQUES AND TERMS

Arrowroot: A fine white powdered starch, similar to corn starch, used to thicken sauces. To use, dissolve the arrowroot in a little cold water to make a paste (a "slurry"). Whisk the slurry into the simmering liquid to be thickened and cook for 1-2 minutes. The thickening action of the arrowroot will diminish if the liquid continues cooking for a long time after thickening.

Blanch: To cook an ingredient very briefly in boiling water to partially cook it or to set its color. The blanched ingredient should be immediately refreshed in cold water to halt the cooking process.

Blind-bake: To pre-bake an empty pastry crust, either partially or completely. A crust should be blind-baked to keep the filling from sogging the pastry, to avoid overcooking a delicate filling that requires only a short time in the oven, or to cook the crust of a pie with an unbaked filling. To blind-bake a crust, line the pan with the dough in the usual manner, then place a circle of parchment paper or wax paper on the dough large enough to cover the bottom and come up the sides. Fill the bottom with pie weights, dried beans or rice—this will prevent the crust from puffing up and cracking during cooking. Bake until partially or completely done, then remove the paper and weights and proceed with the recipe.

Bouquet garni: An important flavoring element for stocks, soups and sauces that imparts flavor during cooking and is discarded before serving. Wrap a bay leaf, several parsley stems, a sprig of fresh thyme and a stick of celery in a leek green and tie into a cylindrical bundle with kitchen twine. Alternatively, wrap the ingredients in cheesecloth instead of the leek. The ingredients may vary according to the recipe.

Chevre: Cheese made from goat's milk, most commonly sold fresh with a slightly creamy texture and mild taste, but also available dried with a more pungent aroma and nutty flavor.

Chiffonade: A method of evenly cutting flat flexible ingredients, such as leafy greens, into long strips. Stack several leaves or slices together, then roll into a cigar shape, cut crosswise into the desired width and unroll.

Clarified butter: Pure butterfat, extracted from regular butter, used frequently for sautéing and frying because it can tolerate higher temperatures than regular butter without burning. To clarify butter melt and boil the butter for several minutes until the milk solids separate from the butterfat, then skim off any surface foam and pour off the butterfat, leaving the milky solids in the bottom of the pan. Discard all but the pure butterfat.

Coulis: A smooth, pourable puree used as a sauce, usually made from fruit or vegetables.

Cucumber—to peel and seed: Scrape away the peel with a vegatable peeler. Cut the cucumber in half lengthwise and with a small teaspoon, scrape out the seeds. The cucumber may now be sliced or diced according to the recipe.

Deglaze: To dissolve the caramelized juices left in the bottom of a pan after sautéing or roasting an ingredient by adding liquid, such as vinegar, stock or wine, and stirring over the heat. The method is often used in making sauces.

Degorge: To sprinkle the cut flesh of an ingredient, such as eggplant, with salt and leave it for 20-30 minutes to draw out excess moisture and bitter juices. The salt and moisture are then wiped off and the ingredient prepared according to the recipe.

Dice: To cut ingredients into a cube shape, generally ranging in size from 1/2-inch square to 1/8-inch square (the very small dice is also known as brunoise). To dice an ingredient, first cut it into julienne strips the correct width, then turn the strips crosswise and cut evenly into dice.

Double boiler: A two-part pan used for cooking delicate ingredients such as chocolate or egg yolks. The top half holds the ingredients to be cooked; it is set over the bottom half, which holds a few inches of water, thereby keeping the ingredients from direct contact with the heat. A double boiler can be improvised easily with a regular saucepan and a snug-fitting stainless steel bowl.

Glace de viande: An intensely flavored syrupy paste made by a long reduction of veal stock, used primarily to flavor sauces; also known as meat glaze. A glaze can also be made from chicken or fish stock (glace de volaille, glace de poisson).

Greenbrier peaches: Large freestone peaches grown in California. They are packed in sweetened peach puree, frozen and canned for The Greenbrier. Very ripe fresh peaches or good quality canned peaches may be substituted for them in most recipes.

Julienne: To cut ingredients into even strips, generally about 2 inches long and varying in width from very fine to about 1/4 inch. For a thick ingredient, such as a carrot, first cut flat slices, then cut the slices into strips, and trim to the desired length. To cut a flat ingredient, such as a slice of ham, simply cut into strips and cut the strips to the desired length.

Leeks—to clean: Leeks tend to be very sandy and require careful attention when cleaning. Slice off most of the tough green leaves and the hairy root. Slice the leek lengthwise, keeping the root end intact if the leek is to be used whole, or cutting all the way through if the leek is to be chopped or sliced. Rinse the leek in cold water, separating it layer by layer to remove the imbedded grit.

Oyster sauce: A prepared sauce with a sweet and salty flavor, containing oyster extract; it is used in some Asian cuisines.

Pastry blender: A utensil for cutting fat into flour in pastry recipes, consisting of a handle and curved stiff wires, shaped somewhat like a stirrup.

Pastry cutter: A utensil for stamping shapes out of rolled-out dough, available in many sizes and shapes with either straight or fluted cutting edges (also called a cookie cutter).

Peppers—to core and seed: Cut around the core with a sharp paring knife and pull to remove it. Slice the pepper in half lengthwise, then shave off the whitish interior ribs. Shake or scrape away any remaining seeds. The pepper may now be sliced or diced according to the recipe.

Peppers—to roast: Preheat the broiler. Place the peppers on a baking sheet and broil close to the heat, turning the peppers as necessary until charred and blistered on all surfaces. Transfer them to a plastic bag and leave until cool enough to handle, at least 10 minutes. The steam created in the bag will enable the skins to slip off easily. Peel off all the skin, remove and discard the core and all the seeds.

Phyllo dough: A very thin, delicate pastry, used traditionally in Middle Eastern cuisines, generally sold frozen. To use phyllo dough, transfer it from the freezer to the refrigerator the day before it is to be used, then take the box from the refrigerator and leave at room temperature about 1 hour before use. Gently unwrap the dough, which consists of a stack of rectangular sheets, and lay it on a dry work surface. Cover the surface of the dough with a very lightly dampened dish cloth. Remove the cloth, peel off one sheet of dough at a time, and use according to the recipe.

Poach: To cook an ingredient gently in a simmering (not boiling) liquid, such as water or stock, often infused with herbs, wine and other flavorings. The method is most appropriate for delicate items such as fish and eggs.

Reduce: To simmer or boil a liquid so it evaporates, reduces in volume and concentrates in flavor. The method is often used in making sauces.

Roux: A mixture of flour and fat, usually butter, cooked together until smooth and the raw flour taste is cooked out. It is used to thicken sauces and soups. A roux may be cooked to varying degrees according to use, such as a light roux for a white sauce and a dark roux for a gravy or gumbo.

Sauté: To cook an ingredient in a shallow pan with a small amount of fat over high heat so the ingredient is quickly browned on the outside and stays moist on the inside.

Sear: To cook an ingredient in a shallow pan with little or no oil over very high heat or in a very hot oven in order to quickly and thoroughly brown the outside. The method is most often used as a preliminary step to another cooking method, such as stewing, though an ingredient may be completely cooked by searing.

Shrimp—to peel and devein: This is easier with raw shrimp, but the same technique is applied to cooked shrimp, too. With your fingers, peel off the shell, leaving the tail on or discarding it, as called for in the recipe. Grasp the shrimp firmly between thumb and forefinger, and with a sharp paring knife make a shallow incision along the back, following the line of the vein if it is visible. Pull or scrape out the vein and discard; rinse the shrimp gently with cool water.

Simmer: To cook a liquid such as a soup (or an ingredient in a liquid, such as a chicken) at just below the boiling point, so the liquid bubbles and trembles but does not boil. This gentle cooking method reduces evaporation and keeps the ingredients tender.

Spatzle press: A utensil used to shape spatzle noodles, usually consisting of a perforated plate through which the dough is pressed by another plate.

Tomatoes—to peel, seed and chop: To remove the skin from a tomato, cut out the core, make a small criss-cross slit in the opposite end and plunge into boiling water for a few seconds, until the edges of the skin begin to come loose. Run the tomato under cold water to stop the cooking and peel off the skin with a knife. To seed the tomato, cut in half crosswise and gently squeeze out the seeds and pulp, leaving only the firm red flesh. At this point the tomato may be cut into strips and chopped or diced according to the recipe.

Virginia ham: A ham made by traditional methods of dry-curing and salting. The ham must be soaked overnight and scrubbed, then simmered for several hours before eating. The most well-known Virginia ham is the Smithfield ham.

Water bath: A flat pan of hot water in which the container holding the ingredient is placed during cooking in order to modify the heat. A water bath is used especially for egg custards and other fragile mixtures, and may be used on top of the stove or in the oven; it is also used to keep delicate items warm. Also called bain marie.

Wild mushrooms — to clean and prepare: Fresh wild mushrooms tend to be very porous and should not be soaked if possible. If the mushrooms appear clean, a careful brushing with a mushroom or pastry brush to remove dust will be adequate. If the mushrooms are dirty, rinse them quickly in a bowl of cold water, lifting them out and allowing the dirt and twigs to sink to the bottom. Lay them on a towel and pat gently to squeeze out the excess water. Trim off any mold or tough spots, such as the stems of shiitakes. Dried wild mushrooms need to be reconstituted and rinsed of grit and dust before use, by soaking in a bowl of very hot water until plump, about 20 minutes. Lift the plump mushrooms out of the soaking water, leaving the grit behind, and dry gently on a towel.

Zest of citrus fruit — to pare or grate: For pared zest, scrape off a strip using a vegetable peeler or sharp paring knife, taking care to omit as much of the white pith as possible. If the zest is to be cut into julienne and used as a garnish, it must be tenderized after cutting by blanching for 2 minutes. For grated zest, grate the peel off the whole fruit using the small holes on a metal grater, scraping off only the colored peel and not the white pith, or scrape off the peel with a zesting tool.

Index

Photography Credits

Thank you to everyone listed below who lent us props for photography.

Sun-Dried Tomato and Chevre Dip: wine glasses, Ann Tate Bell; bowl and platter, Ceramica

Greenbrier Quiche: basket, Ann Tate Bell

Caramelized Brie: wine glasses, Carleton Varney at The Greenbrier

Seafood Gazpacho: wine glass, Keith H. Knost Fine Gifts; plate and bowl, Wolfman Gold & Good Company

Five-Onion Soup: bowl, spoons, wood panel, Betty Alfenito

Greenbrier Two-Bean Chili: mineral water bottle, Linda and Hal Walls

Oven-Roasted Tomato, salad garnished with: plate, Keith H. Knost Fine Gifts

Chevre in Phyllo Pastry, salad garnished with: glass, Wolfman Gold & Good Company; plate and bowl, Hannah Milman

Salmon and Sturgeon in Caviar Butter Sauce: plate, Carleton Varney at The Greenbrier; salt dish (with caviar), Wolfman Gold & Good Company; napkin, Anita Calero

Allegheny Mountain Trout: napkin, Betty Alfenito

Poached Black Bass with Red Pepper Coulis: plate, glasses, vase, candle holder, Keith H. Knost Fine Gifts

Kate's Mountain Barbecued Shrimp: books, Orvis & Kate's Mountain Outfitters; beer glass, Keith H. Knost Fine Gifts

Pan-Seared Scallops on Red Onion Marmalade: plates, napkins, cutlery, Pierre Deux; wine glasses, salt and pepper shakers, Wolfman Gold & Good Company; bird cage, Crabtree & Evelyn

Southern Fried Chicken: plates, Wolfman Gold & Good Company; napkins, Pierre Deux; glasses, Carleton Varney at The Greenbrier; basket, Ann Tate Bell

Roast Chicken Breast Greenbrier Valley: wine glasses, vase, Keith H. Knost Fine Gifts

Herb-Scented Roast Chicken: plates, platter, terrine, candlesticks, Wolfman Gold & Good Company

Turkey Scallopini with Black Bean Relish: wine glasses, Ann Tate Bell

Roast Quail Stuffed with Savoy Cabbage, Wild Rice and Mushrooms: plates, wine glasses, cutlery, salt and pepper shakers, Keith H. Knost Fine Gifts; blanket, Betty Alfenito

New York Strip With Shallot, Lemon, Pepper Crust and Whole-Grained Mustard Sauce: plate, Carleton Varney at The Greenbrier; cutlery, Anita Calero; napkin, Hannah Milman

Veal Fricassee a la Rusch: tureen, plate, Keith H. Knost Fine Gifts; napkin, Betty Alfenito

The Tavern Broiled Veal Chops with Morel Sauce: napkin, Wolfman Gold & Good Company

Broiled Pork Chops with Dried Cherry Compote: water jug, plates, serving bowls, Linda and Hal Walls; wine glasses, Ann Tate Bell; cutlery and serving spoon, Betty Alfenito

Venison Ragout with Pinot Noir and Lingonberries: plates, bowls, cutlery, napkins, wine glasses, tureen, Pierre Deux

Vegetable Ragout with Wild Mushroom Butter: plates, wine glasses, Wolfman Gold & Good Company; ladle, Hannah Milman

Parsnip Puree: water jug, bowl, Linda and Hal Walls; wine glass, Ann Tate Bell

Chevre Souffle: Greenbrier Dairy milk bottle, Linda and Hal Walls; cloth, Betty Alfenito

Corn Bread, Dorothy's Popovers, Zucchini Bread: tongs, Linda and Hal Walls; plate and butter dish, Wolfman Gold & Good Company; knife, Carleton Varney at The Greenbrier

Pecan Bread: tea strainer, cup and saucer, Anita Calero

Pumpkin Muffins: glass, Ann Tate Bell; bowl, plate, napkin, Betty Alfenito

Classic Cheesecake: cake stand, Ann Tate Bell; cups and saucers, Keith H. Knost Fine Gifts

Frozen Grand Marnier Mousse in Almond Lace Cookie Cups: plate, Keith H. Knost Fine Gifts

Greenbrier "Daley" Bread Pudding with Vanilla Sauce and Peach Coulis: plate, Tod Hanger

Double Chocolate Pâté: plate, napkin, Betty Alfenito; glass, Keith H. Knost Fine Gifts; cloth, Hannah Milman

PHOTOGRAPHY IDENTIFICATION

Except where otherwise noted, all historical illustrations and photography are from The Greenbrier archives. Picture page 7 courtesy North Carolina Museum. Photo page 26, bottom, courtesy Lisa Larsen; photo page 27, bottom, courtesy Howard Skidmore. All contemporary location photography is by Jack Mellott except photos pages 29 and 31, Paul Beswick; photo page 38, right, The Greenbrier; photo page 38, bottom, Michael Wyatt.

Credits

Editor: Martha Holmberg

Historical text: Robert S. Conte

Food photography: Ellen Silverman

Location photography: Jack Mellott

Photography assistance: Marianne Smith, Tina West, Jon Naiman

Food stylist: Keith Coughenour, C.C.

Assistant food stylist: Michele Koeniger

Recipe development: Martha Holmberg, Keith Coughenour, C.C., Eric Crane,
Steve Mengel, Scott Bennett

Recipe testing: Carol Mann Herrick, Michele Koeniger, Erryn Shephard, Sherri Talbott Wong

Copyediting: Laura Garrett

Design and production: Rodney Dempsey, Progress Printing

Publishing consultant: Thomasson-Grant

Color separations, printing, binding: Progress Printing

GREENBRIER and COTTAGES
ite Sulphur Springs. W. Va.

WHITE SULPHUR SPRINGS

Announcing
of
The Gre

Greenbrier
West

MENU

Oysters   Hors d'Oeuvres 1 00
Fruit Supreme 75   Olives 30

eine 40   Petite Marmite, Parisienne 50
Green Turtle Soup au Madere 60

oiled Chicken Halibut, Sauce Mousseline 1 00
uery 1 10   Baked Oysters a l'Ancienne 1 00

hicken a la Maryland 1 75
Virginia Ham Baked in Cider with Spinach 1 25
Sweetbread, under glass, Eugenie 1 50
Mignon, Greenbrier 1 75   Spring Lamb Chops, Maison d'Or 1 40

Cranberry Sauce

Astrakhan Caviar   Ho
Radishes 30   Spring
French Sardines 75—La
COCKTAILS—Crab Flake
OYSTERS and CLAMS—

Cream of Broccolli a
Green Turtle

esh Lobster in
Rainbo
Gr
rab Flakes

am wi
n a

unt Verno
— CHO

Segments

ORK, A
HICK
F

July Fourth
NINETEEN HUNDRED FORTY-EIGHT

Casino Luncheon

Puree of Tomatoes aux Croutons   Tomato Juice   Cold Consomme in Jelly

Fried Scallops with Bacon and Sauce Tartare   Beef Hash Browned with Fried Egg
Virginia Corned Beef Hash Browned with Fried Egg
Grilled Combination Spring Lamb C

COLD BUFFET

Tomato Stuffed with Crab Flakes and Watermelon Relish
Roast Turkey with Waldorf Salad and Cr
Sirloin of Beef with String
Fantaisie   Black Raspberry Tart

French Bread

LA VARENNE AT THE GREENBRIER

ESSENCE of FENNEL

FARM RAISED STRIPED BASS
Sauvignon Blanc, Greenbrier Vineyards, Napa Valley, 1988
A Robert Pecota Selection, Napa Valley, 1988

CHENIN BLANC SORBET

TRUFFLED GUINEA HEN BREAST AND SAUSAGE
Wild Mushroom and Apple Sauce
Bordeaux, Clos de la Cure, St. Emilion,
Grand Cru Classe, 1986

SEASONAL SELECTED SALAD GREENS
ROQUEFORT CRISP
Balsamic Vinaigrette

LEMON GRATIN
Muscat Blanc, Robert Pecota, Muscato Di Andrea,
Napa Valley, 1989   DEMI TASSE

GREENBRIER TRUFFLES and CHOCOLATES

Thursday, February 28

Crystal Room
THE GREENBRIER